Live as Heroes

Live
as
Heroes

by

Derek Meyer

First Printing: 2019

ISBN   978-0-359-56020-2

Author: Derek Meyer

Email: derekmeyer.nycity@yahoo.com

Cover/Illustration: Derek Meyer, Rex Lott

About the Author

Author Derek Meyer grew up in Germany and moved to London in 2001, after completing his studies. He eventually fulfilled his lifelong dream and relocated to New York in 2009.

Derek Meyer has worked for different investment banks in both London and New York and has been actively involved in fundraising and supporting the fight against AIDS since his arrival in the States. Derek lives in Chelsea, Manhattan and welcomed his daughter in his life in December 2014.

Meyer has been a keen supporter of several dance companies including the Debbie Allen Dance Academy in Los Angeles and the New York City Ballet with this daughter currently attending ballet lessons at the Jacqueline Kennedy Onassis School by American Ballet Theater.

The author's debut novel "Coming Out in New York" was published in 2012 and followed by his second book "Fame, Baby & Inspiration" in 2014.

Almost five years later he returns with his new book "Lives as Heroes", which gave him the opportunity to write about both the fight against HIV/AIDS and his admiration for the performing arts.

Dedication

    I would like to dedicate this book to my daughter Bella, who already cares so much about the people around her at her young age and who is the light of my life.

    I have no doubt that Bella will be lovely and amazing no matter what she decides to do one day and I am grateful that we both share the ambition to help others and love for the ballet.

    And it would be nice to run that AIDS Run in New York City together in a couple of years. (-:

Acknowledgements

I really want to thank all my friends and colleagues, who have always supported my fundraising activities and who have shown so much interest in my new book during the last months.

And I also want to thank my dear friend Debbie, who invited my daughter and myself to that amazing event at the Apollo Theater on November 30th, 2018 which inspired me to write this book

Introduction

Some of us are told our whole life that we are destined for greatness based solely on the virtue of our names and that sacrifice is for the foolish and survival is all that matters. But I found myself at a crossroad a long time ago when I had to decide what is right. There is no such thing as destiny. Legacies must be earned by the choices we make. I now know that we write our own endings and that we can choose to either hide as villains and cowards or live as heroes.

Certain people had an impact on the man I ultimately became. A handful of them showed me that one of the most amazing things about us is when we possess the ability to take all the pain and all the loss, which we have suffered and turn it into drive, drive to make things better. And then there are those who dedicate their lives to the fight against HIV and AIDS. They continue to find joy in their work and manage to share that joy through the spirit of making a difference, and the possibility of hope right in the face of darkness and despite all that, they have lost.

I am profoundly grateful for the lessons I have learned from the people, who managed to inspire me. I will always remember them as the fighters in the times of AIDS, which include those famous dance artists from the past, who had given HIV and AIDS a face in the early days of the crisis, which saved generations of us later on. And while I was standing at the window of our living room in our new apartment on 21st Street in Chelsea, New York on that rainy day in November 2018 I started to remember all those years, which were defined by both the fight against AIDS and the passion for the arts.

My daughter Bella and I had moved into our new home just a few days earlier and were both looking forward to a night out at the historic Apollo Theater in Harlem to commemorate World AIDS Day. The evening at the Apollo Theater was also expected to be a celebration of dance and creativity and tribute to the legendary icons of dance that have died due to complications from AIDS including Alvin Ailey, Rudolf Nureyev, Ulysses Dove, Michael Peters, Michael Bennett, and Gene Anthony Ray. [1]

Just a few hours before the 30th World AIDS Day my little girl was sleeping in her bedroom surrounded by unpacked boxes, while I had to think about the actual meaning of World AIDS Day, which was designated on December 1st every year since 1988 and which was dedicated to raising awareness of the AIDS pandemic caused by the spread of HIV infection. And I realized how my existence had been impacted by AIDS, which has killed between 28.9 million and 41.5 million people worldwide and which has become one the of the most important global public health issues in recorded history with an estimated 36.7 million people living with HIV. [2]

The world has changed, and society has changed since the news of AIDS first came out back in the early '80s. But even if some of us became the men and women for the modern age free to live, free to love and free to break away the fight against HIV and AIDS remains a war which hasn't been won yet. And suddenly I felt that pain and sadness and remembered those beloved ones who I had lost to AIDS myself.

I closed my eyes for a moment and took a deep breath. Love hurts especially when we lose it and when it is taken away from us. When it happened to me, I was afraid that I would never fully recover from it and be able to love the same way again. Yes, that one was one of the very few loves in my life.

And while many of the guests of the Apollo Theaters were looking forward to a powerful evening filled with moving tributes and extraordinary performances, I sensed that this evening would have an impact on my life and within a blink of an eye the past felt so close like never before.

---

[1] https://www.looktothestars.org/news/18522-ahf-partners-with-legend-debbie-allen-to-present-keeping-the-promise-1000000-lives-in-care-celebrating-icons-of-dance
[2] https://en.wikipedia.org/wiki/World_AIDS_Day

I felt nervous and walked away from the window. My daughter was still sleeping when I closed the bathroom door behind me. I turned the water on and cooled my face. My heart was beating faster.

I felt dizzy, and all those emotions and memories were back and all around me. And then when I dried my face with a towel and looked into the mirror, I suddenly looked into that little boy`s face, who had grown up in the '80s being both fascinated by the power of the performing arts and scared of the deadly disease AIDS.

AIDS in the 1980s – The dark years

Back in 1983 when I washed my face and looked into the mirror after a long day in the fields of the farm, I was a nine years old boy. I was the son of a farmer, who ruled his little kingdom with an iron fist, which he didn`t hesitate to use against his firstborn son, whom he had held responsible for being pushed into early marriage at the age of 20. The "farmer" considered his second son as the wanted one, and I learned from a very young age on the real meaning of discrimination. And I had to experience in a harsh way that being different was not something, which was desired in the community I grew up in.

While "the farmer" and my brother were the same ruthless and ignorant people who put the farm, money and their interests before family and moral values my mother turned out to be the real opportunist in that family. "The opportunist" kept supporting the stronger members in her family and stand by her man even when he treated his flesh and blood like a dog on the fields of his farm.

The opportunist looked away back in the 1980s, and she continued doing that until to this day. She never questioned the meaning of right and wrong and turned into a bitter woman some 33 years later when she found herself being alone and left behind by those, who she failed to protect in her family at an earlier stage.

I will never forget the day when the "farmer" and the "opportunist" showed their real colors, which consequently ended my childhood. And I will always remember the day when I first learned about AIDS back in the early 1980s.

The news from the AIDS crisis in the States affected me even when I was that young boy on that farm in Germany, who didn`t seem to know much about life. But deep down I already sensed back then the threat, which was coming from HIV and AIDS and that I had to ask myself the question if I wanted to get involved in the fight against AIDS or not.

The beginning of the AIDS crisis in America

Many scientists believe that the earliest form of HIV spread from chimpanzees to humans before 1931 when hunters had contact with animal blood in Africa. But it took nearly three decades before researchers found the earliest case of HIV blood sample of a man from the Democratic Republic of Congo, who died in 1959. The disease spread very slowly in its early years, but records list a case in the United States of America, when a 49-year-old shipping clerk from Haiti died in New York City on June 28th, 1959 of Pneumocystis carinii pneumonia, which is a disease closely associated to AIDS. [3] [4] [5]

But how did the actual AIDS crisis in the United States start? Many researchers suggest that the HIV strain that started the North American pandemic had found its way to the USA in the late 1970s via Zaire and Haiti. The sexual revolution was in full swing in those years, and HIV was spreading silently within the gay communities in the large cities in the States. Ken Horne from San Francisco would be identified as the first victim of the AIDS epidemic in the United States later on when he was reported to the Center for Diseases Control and Prevention with Kaposi`s sarcoma and died on April 24th, 1980. [6]

But there are other theories. Many people from Haiti were working in the Congo in the 1960s, and genetic studies indicate that the actual HIV virus first arrived in the Americas in 1966, when it affected one person in Haiti. This thesis, however, is also contradicted with the death of the 16-year-old teenager Robert Rayford from St. Louis in 1969, who became the alleged first known AIDS death in the United States at a time when it took the

---

[3] https://evolution.berkeley.edu/evolibrary/news/081101_hivorigins
[4] Pence GE (2008). "Preventing the Global Spread of AIDS". Medical Ethics Accounts of the Cases That Shaped and Define Medical Ethics. New York, NY: McGraw-Hill. p. 330.
[5] Hennigar, G.R., Vinijchaikul, K., Roque, A.L, Lyons, H.A. (1 April 1961). "Pneumocystis carinii Pneumonia in an Adult. Report of a Case". American Journal of Clinical Pathology. 35 (4): 353–364
[6] Solved: the mystery of how AIDS left Africa," New Scientist, November 3, 2007, p.20

HIV at least ten years to develop into AIDS. Robert Rayford had never left the Midwest and never received a blood transfusion. [7]

The years before AIDS were described by many as the "Golden Age of Promiscuity." Gay activism and gay life had exploded across the entire country since gay men had fought back against a police raid at a bar in New York`s Greenwich Village in 1969, which were well known as the Stonewall Riots.

People were enjoying free sex to the fullest and were not worried about the risks in the time of available birth control pills, legalized abortion and developed antibiotics for sexually transmitted diseases. People were having fun across the country, and gay men were walking carefree hand in hand on the streets of New York City and living their freedom. [8]

But it turned out that the new-found free sex came at a very high price when the dermatologist and virologist Dr. Alvin Friedman-Kien met Larry Kramer and a dozen of other gay men at Kramer`s apartment near Washington Square Park and informed them about a mysterious illness that seemed to target gay men. Friedman-Kien used terms such as Kaposi`s sarcoma and described the new disease as some gay cancer, which appeared to be related to a gay sexual activity which outraged the group. But although the men were not keen on the idea to give up their new-found freedom and free love, they already sensed the possibility of a significant health crisis and were aware that something had to be done. [9]

Nowadays it is well established that the HIV virus traveled from the tropical regions of Central Africa to the United States of America and after a few earlier unsuccessful attempts became a national and global pandemic targeting those communities first, which the straight world preferred not to see. When a patient overheard his doctor mentioning some gay men being treated in intensive care units in New York for a strange form of pneumonia

[7] KQED LGBT Timeline. Kqed.org. Retrieved on 2011-12-03.
[8] https://ew.com/article/1996/07/19/golden-age-promiscuity/
[9] https://propertibazar.com/article/hiv-history-nsw-perspective-acon_5a8f6697d64ab2b073c606d2.html

it was Lawrence Mass who received a tip and became the first journalist in the world to publish a story about AIDS in a newspaper. Lawrence Mass article "Disease Rumors Largely Unfounded" about the epidemic appeared in the gay newspaper New York Native on May 18th, 1981 and repeated the public health official's claims that there was no disease targeting the gay community in New York City. [10]

The Center for Diseases Control and Prevention ("CDC") published a report and made the public aware of a high number of cases of Kaposi's sarcoma and Pneumocystis in California and New York City. It turned out that the government agency had already been gathering information about the outbreak for one month at the time when Lawrence Mass article was published. [11]

It took further time before the government noted quietly and discretely that something was happening when a Morbidity and Mortality Weekly Report was released on June 5th, 1981. The report stated that in the period October 1980 to May 1981 5 young homosexual men were treated for Pneumocystis Carinii Pneumonia at three different hospitals in Los Angeles, California and that two of the patients had died. [12]

When the government chose to stay silent in the absence of the promised vaccine AIDS activists started to provide care for AIDS patients who were falling ill. Larry Kramer and five other gay men took the brave step to found Gay Men's Health Crisis back in New York City in January 1982, which would be known as the oldest HIV/AIDS service organization and first provider of HIV/AIDS prevention in the world later on. The name of the organization made an explicit reference to the target population of gay men and seemingly temporary nature of the disease. [13]

---

[10] Kinsella, James (1989). Covering the Plague: AIDS and the American Media. Rutgers University Press. p. 28. ISBN 9780813514826.

[11] www.cdc.gov/mmwr/pdf/wk/mm5021.pdf

[12] Centers for Disease Control (June 1981). "Pneumocystis pneumonia--Los Angeles" (PDF). MMWR. Morbidity and Mortality Weekly Report. 30 (21): 250–2. PMID 6265753

[13] https://www.hiv.gov/hiv-basics/overview/history/hiv-and-aids-timeline

The GMHC met in people's living rooms and faced some challenges in the early years when they aimed to achieve ambitious goals in a time of plenty of uncertainty in the 1980s. The GMHC tried to promote prevention without being aware of what caused the disease; they were lacking the financial resources to back research and struggled to sustain patients with the disease since there were no effective treatments available. [14]

Another issue was that the GMHC felt profoundly disconnected from mainstream and failed to get the attention and funding from the government including the New York Public Health System. The GMHC's disco parties didn't raise enough funds for research either, and Friedman-Kien and other scientists relied on handouts and private foundations since it seemed that the disease targeted only gay men and junkies until hemophiliacs developed PCP pneumonia and other opportunistic infections. [15]

Fortunately, things started to change when Robert Bazell presented the news on NBC Nightly News in June 1982. Mr. Bazell informed the public that it seemed that some infectious agent was causing the disease, which was the first news report about the illness on Television. Shortly afterward gay community leaders, federal bureaucrats and the Center for Diseases Control and Prevention proposed for the first time the term AIDS (acquired immune deficiency syndrome) in Washington on July 27th, 1982, which replaced GRID (gay-related immune deficiency) with highlighting that this disease was not gay specific. [16]

At that time the country had believed for a long time that people living with AIDS were solely gay people. When co-founder of Gay Men's Health Crisis and activist Larry Kramer questioned host Jane Pauley in a 1983 NBC's "Today" show, if

[14] http://www.cnn.com/2011/HEALTH/05/25/edmund.white.hiv.aids/index.html
[14] http://www.cnn.com/2011/HEALTH/05/25/edmund.white.hiv.aids/index.html
[15] https://www.youtube.com/watch?v=1LKJ5ZzzL0w
[16] https://www.queerty.com/rare-1983-larry-kramer-interview-offers-a-glimpse-at-his-role-as-an-outspoken-activist-20140527

she could imagine what it must be like if she had lost 20 of her friends in 18 months and she responded with "No", it described the significant problem, not just at the beginning of the AIDS crisis. The majority of the population in the United States just failed to relate to the disease, understand its severity and sympathize with its victims. [17]

In January 1983 Francoise Barre-Sinoussi from the Pasteur Institute in Paris managed to isolate a retrovirus which killed T-cells from the lymph of a gay man and hemophiliac sufferers. The virus was called several names and eventually named HIV in 1986. [18]

When it was reported that the virus was replicating in the bloodstreams of hemophiliacs, who had received contaminated blood transfusions and injection users, the media subsequently named people who were exposed to HIV infections as members of the "Four-H Club." The Four-H Club included hemophiliacs, homosexual men, heroin users, and Haitians or people of Haitian origin since many cases were reported in Haiti at that time. But not just the average American people but also leading politicians continued to call AIDS the "Gay Plaque." [19]

The public perception of AIDS impacted the lives of so many gay people not only living and fighting AIDS in big cities such as New York or Los Angeles but also those who were growing up and being afraid of the consequences of their Coming Outs in a rather scary and uncertain time.

How did the government handle the AIDS crisis back in the 1980s?

The gay community had achieved so much in between the Stonewall Riots in 1969, and the early 1980s and activists continued to push for civil rights advances and municipal and

---

[18] And The Band Played On, Randy Shilts, p. 227, St. Martin's Press, 2007
[19] http://www.microbiologybook.org/lecture/4hclub.htm

state-level protections against discrimination in some public employment. Roughly two dozen states had decriminalized homosexuality as sodomy by 1980, and some LGBTQ activists were already discussing the legal recognition for gay marriage, what actually wouldn`t happen before Barack Obama`s time as the first African American president of the United States some 30 years later. [20]

But the LGBTQ civil rights movement faced a significant backlash when the public learned about the first HIV cases in New York and Los Angeles. Evangelic Christian leaders delivered a petition to then-president Jimmy Carter and demanded a halt to the advance of gay rights and stated that "God's judgment is going to fall on America as on other societies that allowed homosexuality to become a protected way of life". [21]

But what did the government in the country do to support the fight against AIDS in the early days? There were 853 AIDS deaths in the USA by 1982. But the hopes of LGBTQ activists that the growing medical crisis would get more attention from the government were ignored with the election of Moral Majority ally Ronald Reagan. Reagan`s press secretary Larry Speakes shocked activists when he described AIDS just as a gay plaque and laughed loudly in a White House Briefing on October 15th, 1982 when asked about whether the president of the United States was tracking the spread of AIDS.

By 1983 the number had climbed up to 2,304 AIDS deaths in the USA and Larry Speakes and journalists were still cracking jokes about AIDS in a White House Briefing on June 13th, 1983. Many activists had described the president`s actions as questionable when Ronald Reagan suggested that gay men should cut down on cruising.

---

[20] https://www.nbcnews.com/feature/nbc-out/lgbtq-history-month-early-days-america-s-aids- crisis- n919701
[21] https://www.nbcnews.com/feature/nbc-out/lgbtq-history-month-early-days-america-s-aids- crisis- n919701

By 1984 4,251 people had died of AIDS in the USA, and when another White House Briefing took place on December 11th, 1984 the Center for Diseases Control and Prevention had already published a report that an estimated 300,000 people had been exposed to AIDS. And even if all the news were out there the president's press secretary still claimed that he hadn't heard anything about president Ronald Reagan planning on doing something about AIDS and expressed no opinion about the pandemic. [22]

When Larry Speakes retired from public services in 1987, he was awarded the Presidential Citizens Medal by Ronald Reagan. Speakes admitted in his memoir in the following year that he had manufactured quotes that were later attributed to the president and shortly afterward resigned from his position as a vice president for communications with investment bank Merrill Lynch. [23]

On April 23rd, 1984 the Health and Human Services Secretary Margaret Heckler announced at a press conference the probable discovery of the cause of AIDS by American scientist Robert Gallo, which was caused by the retrovirus "human immunodeficiency" which was called HIV. Ms. Heckler pointed out that the development of an AIDS test was on the way and forecasted the availability of a vaccine by 1986. [24]

The FDA approved the first commercially available HIV test ELISA on March 2nd, 1985 but the vaccine never arrived. It took President Ronald Reagan an additional six months before he finally used the word AIDS on September 17th, 1985, when a reporter raised a question regarding the lack of medical research funding during a press conference.

Many people criticized that Ronald Reagan should have taken that step years ago at in the early stages of the epidemic and not in a time when the number of AIDS deaths had climbed

[22] https://www.youtube.com/watch?v=yAzDn7tE1lU
[23] https://en.wikipedia.org/wiki/Larry_Speakes
[24] https://www.nbcnews.com/feature/nbc-out/lgbtq-history-month-early-days-america-s-aids-crisis-n919701

up to over 12,000 Americans, and the virus had already spread through hemophiliacs and injection drug users. And it became evident that everyone including well-established actors and household names could develop AIDS, when actor Rock Hudson died of AIDS on October 2nd, 1985 who the first celebrity was publicly admitting having AIDS. [25] [26]

Activists believed that it happened far too late when the eight-page report "Understanding AIDS" was sent to 107,000,000 households in the United States by Surgeon General C. Everett Koop in 1988. The report was the first federal authority providing explicit advice to US citizens on how they could protect themselves from AIDS. [27]

When Ronald Reagan's former vice president George H.W. Bush died on the evening of Worlds AIDS Day in 2018 many people remembered him for not doing much to end negative attitudes and thoughts about people with AIDS. In a time when the streets of the AIDS epicenter San Francisco felt like a ghost town with the ghosts being still alive, sick people found it hard to talk about AIDS back in the 1980s, which was a shame because talking about AIDS would have helped those suffering from the disease at that time. [28]

Bush had signed the Americans with Disabilities Act in 1990, which also protected people with HIV and the Ryan White Care Act, the largest federally funded program for people living with AIDS. President Bush let countless people who had HIV or Aids down soon after when he stated in 1991 that a way to control AIDS was to change someone's behavior. Bush even added that being gay was not a healthy lifestyle and put himself in line with people who tried to convince others that AIDS was God's punishment and demanded not to show sympathy to the ones who were suffering from AIDS. People still criticize Bush for his

---

[25] https://www.youtube.com/watch?v=yAzDn7tE1lU
[26] https://www.nbcnews.com/feature/nbc-out/lgbtq-history-month-early-days-america-s-aids-crisis-n919701
[27] The C. Everett Koop Papers – AIDS, the Surgeon General, and the Politics of Public Health.nlm.nih.gov
[28] https://abc7news.com/politics/aids-epidemic-survivors-say-bush-wasnt-wonderful-president-to-everyone/4833395/

failure to take on a leadership role and to ask for compassion for gay people and those living with AIDS when he once asked his fellow Americans for being a kinder and gentler nation. [29]

After Larry Kramer left the GMHC, he wrote the play "The Normal Heart" about the early days of Gay Men's Health Crisis and became the man behind the formation of the AIDS Coalition to Unleash Power or ACT UP in New York City. ACT UP's actions are credited for speeding up the government's response to the AIDS crisis and faster testing and treatment of lifesaving drugs.

ACT Up was also well known for being instrumental for shifting public attention to the dangerous and deadly impact of homophobic public health policies with demonstrations taking place on the financial center of the world Wall Street. ACT UP managed to put even more national media attention towards ADIS when taking over St. Patrick's Cathedral in New York City in December 1989 and placing a giant condom over the house of a well-known homophobic senator in North Carolina. [30]

The rise and fall of AZT and the crushed hopes of millions in the 1980s

Long before people were able to choose among more than 40 combination drugs that can treat the disease and keep HIV levels low so that people with HIV would never get sick – there was nothing. [31]

People felt that their needs were being ignored and that medicine and scientists weren't doing enough when the disease heavily attacked the patient's immune systems. They found themselves consequently battling life-threatening AIDS-related illnesses such as Pneumocystis carinii pneumonia, the potential

---

[29] https://abc7news.com/politics/aids-epidemic-survivors-say-bush-wasnt-wonderful-president-to-everyone/4833395/
[30] https://www.nbcnews.com/feature/nbc-out/lgbtq-history-month-early-days-america-s-aids-crisis-n919701
[31] http://time.com/4705809/first-aids-drug-azt/

severe AIDS-related eye infection Cytomegalovirus retinitis, which can lead to blindness, chronic lung diseases or the AIDS-related skin cancer Kaposi`s sarcoma. Other syndromes included significant weight loss, chronic diarrhea or weakness and constant or intermittent fever for at least 30 days. [32]

In 1984 it was established that women could also catch HIV through sexual activities. But just around 3,000 people had been diagnosed with AIDS at that time, and many pharmaceutical companies including Burroughs Wellcome showed little interest in developing a drug against AIDS. [33]

That changed when early forecasts predicted that hundreds of thousands could die within the next years and that millions of people were already infected with HIV. People with HIV were desperate and had incredibly high hopes when the news came out that the U.S. Food and Drug Administration (FDA) approved a drug, which was considered by many as the first weapon against the virus since the discovery of HIV and AIDS. [34]

The government inactivity had virtually totally ignored the arrival of the new disease and failed to take the right actions for years when everyone was suddenly talking about the new drug Azidothymidine ("AZT"). AZT was not an original from scratch developed drug and had instead been abandoned on the shelf since it was initially developed in the 1960s by a U.S. researcher to support the fight against cancer. Back in the 1960s, the original idea of AZT was that the compound inserts itself into the DNA of a cancer cell and manipulate its ability to replicate and produce more cancer cells. [35]

Only a minority of people were aware some twenty years later that AZT hadn`t worked in the first place when it was tested in mice and consequently been put aside in the 1960s. When AIDS emerged as the most talked about infectious disease in the

[32] http://hivinsite.ucsf.edu/insite?page=pb-diag-04-00
[33] https://www.independent.co.uk/arts-entertainment/the-rise-and-fall-of-azt-it-was-the-drug-that-had-to-work-it-brought-hope-to-people-with-hiv-and-2320491.html
[34] http://time.com/4705809/first-aids-drug-azt/
[35] http://time.com/4705809/first-aids-drug-azt/

1980s the pharmaceutical company Burroughs Wellcome from Carolina was desperate to find the first medication that might fight against HIV and started a massive test of potential drugs, which included Compound S, which was another version of the original AZT.

AZT seemed to work and block HIV's activity. Samples were quickly sent to the FDA and National Cancer Institute, who noted the enormous significance of the discovery. At that time the testing of the new drug was expected to take the FDA 8 to 10 years to ensure that the drug was save and indeed stopped the HIV in some way, even if it wouldn't cure people of their HIV infections.

There was a lot of pressure coming from different areas who wanted AZT to hit the markets as soon as possible. Patients who had been diagnosed with HIV grew desperate. And doctors were relieved that there was something better out there than underground and probably life-threatening therapies and they were keen to prescribe a drug to their patients which had passed official tests.

Wellcome sensed the enormous potential revenues which could be created by the first available AIDS medication and people from the government had to react since it was known at that stage that not just homosexual men but also hemophiliacs and drug users had caught HIV. No one wanted to wait for the FDA to test the drug AZT for 8 to 10 years and different groups kept putting the FDA under pressure to fast track the testing of AZT. [36]

But what did the testing involve? To establish, if AZT was safe, the drug was quickly injected into patients, and side effects such as severe intestinal problems, damage to the immune system, nausea, vomiting and headaches deemed as acceptable and AZT considered as relatively safe. But the question, if AZT was effective was supposed to be addressed with a controversial trial which included 282 people who had

---

[36] http://time.com/4705809/first-aids-drug-azt/

26

been diagnosed with AIDS. They were randomly assigned to take either capsules of AZT or sugar pills for six months, and neither doctors nor patients knew, if they were on AZT or not.

It came for many scientists as a surprise when Burroughs Welcome decided after just 16 weeks to stop the trial. The company suddenly announced that there was substantial evidence that AZT was working with one death in one group and 19 deaths in the other group and argued that the continuance of the trial was unethical since it deprived one group of patients of the potentially life-saving treatment. AZT was quickly considered by many as "the light at the end of the tunnel" and approved by the FDA as the first AIDS medication in a record time of just 20 months on March 19, 1987. The drug was about to receive a massive welcome just like the Beatles when they first visited the United States decades earlier. [37]

But how reliable was the actual trial after all? Reports started to surface shortly after the completion of the examination that test patients had also been treated with other medication for health issues, which were associated with AIDS such as pneumonia, diarrhea and other symptoms and the question came up if the suddenly improved results could be credited to AZT alone. [38]

Some patients had even received blood transfusions during the test trial, which had provided them with healthy new blood and an improved capability to fight the virus better. And then there were additional rumors that patients from the 12 centers had switched pills to improve their chances to receive the magic drug instead of the placebo. Other sources suggested that some patients had to be taken off AZT altogether to prevent further damage to their bone marrow and immune systems. [39]

Furthermore, many questions about the drug remained unanswered when it was approved. Neither the FDA nor

[37] http://time.com/4705809/first-aids-drug-azt/
[38] http://time.com/4705809/first-aids-drug-azt/
[39] http://time.com/4705809/first-aids-drug-azt/

Burroughs Wellcome had established for how long the benefit of AZT lasted and if it was an appropriate treatment for those patients who weren't sick yet or for those who were further along in their disease. Overall there was a lot of uncertainty about AZT, but the FDA felt the pressure to release the drug especially because AZT seemed to be the only available drug which was fighting AIDS. AIDS had already turned out to be a growing epidemic in the meantime which was about to crash on the shores of an unsuspecting and unprepared population and take millions of lives. [40]

Once AZT was approved, it was out there and became one of Burrough Wellcome's best selling drugs in the history of the company. AZT seemed unstoppable in 1986, and almost all available funds were channeled to support its development and other alternative potential treatments were not further explored or taken into considerations.

Unfortunately, AZT was only available for those who could afford the drug and activists, and public health officials raised concerns when Burroughs Wellcome was motivated by the enormous financial rewards and offered AZT for about USD 8,000 to USD 10,000 a year. The high costs of the drug made it unaffordable for many uninsured and an already vulnerable population of HIV patients. Larry Kramer and his colleagues from ACT UP were some of the first activists who protested against the pharmaceutical company and the drug AZT's high annual price of USD 10,000 and demanded that the access to affordable health care must be everyone's right, which will be another more detailed topic in this book. [41]

Patients who were prescribed AZT as a treatment for AIDS went through a grueling regime and were required to take the pills every four hours day and night to slow down the progression of the disease. Nowadays it is well known that does not even

---

[40] http://time.com/4705809/first-aids-drug-azt/
[41] https://www.nbcnews.com/feature/nbc-out/lgbtq-history-month-early-days-america-s-aids-crisis-n919701

prevent death and that such high amounts of AZT are toxic overdoses. [42]

To make matters worse people who were taking AZT experienced terrible side effects such as chronic headaches, nausea, heart problems and weight issues and rising HIV levels after some time and were suddenly confronted with a virus, which had mutated to become resistant against the drug. Some patients felt much worse with AZT then they did without it. AZT was considered by some to be effective in treating AIDS, but was it beneficial for those who took it before they became ill? Would AZT keep people alive long enough until maybe a cure was found one day? Was it worth taking a drug, which seemed toxic? [43]

The hopes of millions of patients were crashed when the Anglo-French program Concorde and biggest clinical trial of AZT concluded that early treatment with AZT worked for some patients for some time, who had HIV but not yet developed AIDS. Eight hundred seventy-seven people had received AZT during that trial and 872 were given a placebo over three years, and the overall conclusion was that AZT was a waste of time and made absolutely no difference to either mortality rates or the progression of the disease. The results were shocking when there were 79 AIDS-related deaths in the AZT group compared with 67 in the placebo group. [44]

Before Concorde, everybody wanted to be on AZT, but suddenly questions were raised if the drug`s side effects and all the suffering had been avoidable. The Centers of Diseases Control and Prevention had established that the HIV positive status changes to AIDS when a patient's white blood cell count decreases to 200 which triggered severe infections such as pneumonia, cancer or a wasting syndrome characterized by severe weight loss, diarrhea, and high fever. [45]

[42] https://www.nbcnews.com/feature/nbc-out/lgbtq-history-month-early-days-america-s-aids-crisis-n919701
[43] https://www.independent.co.uk/arts-entertainment/the-rise-and-fall-of-azt-it-was-the-drug-that-had-to-work-it-brought-hope-to-people-with-hiv-and-2320491.html
[44] https://www.independent.co.uk/arts-entertainment/the-rise-and-fall-of-azt-it-was-the-drug-that-had-to-work-it-brought-hope-to-people-with-hiv-and-2320491.html
[45] https://quizlet.com/148238640/med-surg-exam-1-chapter-15-flash-cards/

Many patients experienced that their T4 count and general health improved during the first year with AZT, before they started to get sick, had repeated chest infections or even strokes with the T counts drastically decreasing. It was highlighted that AZT seemed to work well for a maximum of one year before resulting in visible damages. A patient from the UK reported that once he threw away all the pills – 7 in the morning and 7 in the evening, which had to be taken – and changed his diet he started to feel better and experienced a satisfying T4 count. [46] [47] [48]

So was AZT a trap, which almost everyone was falling into? For many people, the AZT dream came to an end, when patients, medical staff, activists and the government had to accept that AZT wasn't the solution when it became apparent that more drugs were needed and advocates started to criticize the FDA for not moving quickly enough to test and approve alternative medications. [49]

---

[46] https://www.independent.co.uk/arts-entertainment/the-rise-and-fall-of-azt-it-was-the-drug-that-had-to-work-it-brought-hope-to-people-with-hiv-and-2320491.html
[47] https://www.nbcnews.com/feature/nbc-out/lgbtq-history-month-early-days-america-s-aids-crisis-n919701
[48] http://time.com/4705809/first-aids-drug-azt/
[49] http://time.com/4705809/first-aids-drug-azt/

Proposition 64

In the absence of a cure and proper medication some groups, which mainly consisted of homophobic members had their ideas, how the AIDS crisis should be approached. They kept pushing for Proposition 64 in 1986, which was a proposition in the State of California on the November 4th, 1986 ballot and an initiative that would have restored AIDS to the list of communicable diseases. Fortunately, the measure was defeated by a margin of 71% to 29%. [50]

Activists associated with Lyndon LaRouche had formed the "Prevent AIDS Now Initiative Committee" (PANIC) and pushed to add AIDS on the list of diseases, which are regulated by the State. The approval of Proposition 64 would have given county health officers the authority to prevent people who have HIV/AIDS from working in schools and as food handlers and provide them with the power to quarantine them if they felt that they exposed a health risk to the general public. [51]

Opponents of the initiative considered the initiative as an effort to force HIV-positive people out of their jobs and into quarantine and health professionals worried that Proposition 64 would severely hurt their ability to treat those patients in need and find a cure for AIDS. The supporters of Proposition 64 however seriously argued that AIDS could be transmitted by insects, respiratory means and casual contacts, which weren`t based on any kind of scientific support. [52]

Activists were anxious that this proposition could pass and planned a torchlight march on the headquarters of Lyndon LaRouche and had the actor's union and political figures with them. The proposal would not pass after all, but the general mood and former possibility of passing highlighted another major issue in the 1980s. [53]

---

[50] https://en.wikipedia.org/wiki/1986_California_Proposition_64
[51] https://www.youtube.com/watch?v=p_2nqK2BoEs
[52] https://en.wikipedia.org/wiki/1986_California_Proposition_64
[53] https://www.youtube.com/watch?v=p_2nqK2BoEs

Discrimination in the '80s

There was a lot of discrimination in the '80s. I was that young boy who cycled 6 miles to school in the morning and 6 miles back home in the afternoon every day because some other cruel teenagers were making cruel jokes on the school bus. Being different and being the son of a wealthy farmer made me an easy target for those kids, who were watching in envy my parent's estate from the school bus every day and were simply jealous of my family's wealth. But the bullies weren't aware of the agony I was going through at that time and what was going on behind those walls of that farm.

I was proud back then, but I tried to avoid certain situations and attacks of those bullies, who were not making the effort to get to know me, while I was very popular with my class mates. I was aware that being different wasn't a good thing in the '80s.

Nowadays I am working very hard as a single parent to provide my daughter with happiness, confidence, and stability. But back then my parents tried constantly to change me. The farmer and the opportunist found great pleasure when they pointed out my shortcomings and compared me with those farming loving cousins of mine who seemed to be copies of their proud fathers. But those relatives also lacked distinctive personalities on their own, which neither set them apart nor made them real heroes later on in life.

When people living with HIV and AIDS shared their stories in magazines or newspapers back in the 1980s, it seemed that their life stopped when they learned about their HIV positive test results and they eventually experienced three of the side effects of AIDS; dementia, diarrhea, and disgrace.

The general population still believed that AIDS could be transmitted via tears or saliva or mosquitoes and limited social contacts and suddenly people didn't want others to pick up their babies and let them kiss on their cheeks. Especially gay people felt isolated before educated people finally managed to get the word out that HIV and AIDS couldn`t be transmitted through non-sexual gestures. But was everyone believing that and how did the straight world feel about gay men? [54]

Many people were arguing that the government didn`t care about homophobic bigotry and instead was sending out the wrong messages. People wanted to turn gay men straight because they believed that was the way to stop AIDS before it would spread to the heterosexual community. A lot of people assumed that all gay people had AIDS and were a potential threat to their health, the health of their children and grandchildren. [55]

School children and teenagers who seemed "different" were attacked on the schoolyards and on their way home and gay people were ridiculed in trashy talk shows and booed out by audiences. Many bars had signs with "faggots stay out," and the gay community was shocked when the college student Matt Sheppard was killed and put up as a scarecrow and left there for 18 hours. [56]

The Geoffrey Bowers Story

The movie "Philadelphia" from 1993 was inspired by attorney Geoffrey Bowers, who found himself being fired from the firm Baker & McKenzie after AIDS-related Kaposi`s sarcoma lesions appeared on his face. His employers stated that Bowers was let go due to performance issues. But the attorney didn`t leave without a fight and sued the firm, which became the first AIDS discrimination case becoming a public hearing. [57]

Geoffrey Bowers was born in Cambridge, Massachusetts on December 29, 1953, and studied political science at Browns

---

[54] http://www.cnn.com/2011/HEALTH/05/25/edmund.white.hiv.aids/index.html
[55] https://www.youtube.com/watch?v=p_2nqK2BoEs
[56] https://www.youtube.com/watch?v=p_2nqK2BoEs
[57] Navarro, Mireya (January 21, 1994), /1994/01/21/nyregion/vindicating-lawyer-with-aids-years-too-late-bias-battle-over-dismissal-
[57] Lawyer With AIDS Charges Job Discrimination", New York Times, July 15, 1987, retrieved 2008-02-25

University and later on law at Benjamin N. Cardozo School of Law in New York City in the fall of 1979. Bowers language skills covered Italian, German, Dutch and Spanish when he joined the international law firm Baker McKenzie in August 1984. When Bowers started experiencing headaches and yellow spots in the following year doctors diagnosed him with meningitis. Geoffrey learned in April 1986 that he was suffering from Kaposi`s sarcoma and AIDS. [58]

His employer dismissed him in July 1986 two months after he was given a satisfactory evaluation without following standard termination procedures, consulting with his supervisors or reviewing his client list or billable hours. Bowers supervisors had objected, but 12 out of 15 partners voted again to dismiss Geoffrey, and he consequently left the law firm on December 5, 1986. [59]

Geoffrey Bowers filed a complaint alleging discrimination with the New York State Division of Human Rights and hearings started on July 14, 1987. He insisted that he had been let go because of the skin lesions that had become visible on his body and face while his former employer stated that there had been performance issues.

It took a total of 6 years to finally resolve the case after hearings took place on 39 days during the first two years. A confidentiality agreement between the law firm and the Bowers family was reached after the agency awarded Bowers USD 500,000 and the back-pay Geoffrey Bowers had earned if he had remained employed.

Geoffrey Bowers passed away two months after the hearing had begun and his long-term partner Alex Londres lost his fight against AIDS one year later. [60]

---

[58] Navarro, Mireya (January 21, 1994), /1994/01/21/nyregion/vindicating-lawyer-with-aids-years-too-late-bias-battle-over-dismissal-proves tml?sec=health&pagewanted=1

[60] Navarro, Mireya (January 21, 1994), /1994/01/21/nyregion/vindicating-lawyer-with-aids-years- too-late-bias-battle-over-dismissal-proves html?sec=health&pagewanted=1
[60] Resnik, Susan (1999). Blood Saga: Hemophilia, AIDS, and the Survival of a

The Ryan White Story

But the discrimination which many young people including myself were dealing with as teenagers was nothing compared with what young Ryan Wayne White had to go through. Nearly 90% of hemophiliacs who were treated with blood clotting factors between 1979 and 1984 were infected with HIV, and Hepatitis C after blood banks and pharmaceutical companies had dismissed calls by the CDC to use Hepatitis B tests as a surrogate until HIV tests became available. [61]

And like so many others the young Ryan White learned that he had been infected with HIV by a blood transfusion which had been part of his regular treatment for hemophilia when doctors performed a partial lung removal and diagnosed Ryan with AIDS on December 17th, 1984. [62]

When parents and faculty members of the public school Western Middle School in Russiaville, Indiana learned about Ryan`s disease, they were trying hard to keep the teenager away from the school premises. When the school`s principal gave in Ryan`s family filed a lawsuit seeking to overturn the ban, which made Ryan a national poster child for HIV/AIDS in the United States who used his sudden celebrity status to become an advocate for AIDS research and public education. [63]

After the Western Middle School in Russiaville refused to let Ryan return to school after he started feeling better the family filed a lawsuit in the U.S. District Court in Indianapolis and an Indiana Department of Education officer ruled that Ryan must be allowed to attend school. 151 of 360 students stayed home when he was permitted to return to school for one day in February

Community. University of California Press. ISBN 978-0-520-21195-7.
[60] White, Ryan; Ann Marie Cunningham (1991). Ryan White: My Own Story. Dial Books. ISBN 978-0-8037-0977-5.
[60] Specter, Michael (September 3, 1985). "AIDS Victim's Right to Attend Public School Tested in Corn Belt". The Washington Post.

1985, and a group of families started an alternative school and withdrew their children when Ryan White was admitted to the school in April 1985. [64]

Threats of violence and lawsuits continued, and the editors of the local newspaper who had supported White editorially and financially were threatened with death. Ryan himself wasn't happy in 8th grade, he didn't have many friends, and the school made him eat with disposable utensils, use separate bathrooms and didn't allow him to attend gym class. The family decided to leave Kokomo and move to the town Cicero in Indiana after a bullet was fired through their living room window.

The teenager was nervous before his first day at Hamilton Heights High School in Arcadia Indiana and positive surprised when the school principal, school system superintendent and a handful of students welcomed him with handshakes. They had been educated about AIDS and were not afraid to shake his hand. [65]

Ryan White had the opportunity to discuss the tribulations with the disease frequently on national television and in newspapers, appeared in educational and fundraising campaigns. The teenager also spoke before the President's Commission on the AIDS Epidemic about the discrimination which he had faced when he first tried to return to middle school in Russiaville but how education about AIDS made him welcome in the new town of Cicero. [66]

Ryan had a small cameo role in the 1989 ABC television movie "The Ryan White Story," which was seen by 15 million viewers. The mayor's office of Kokomo was flooded with complaints after the film had aired, and Ryan White ultimately became one of a handful of visible people with AIDS in the 1980s

[64] Ruling sends AIDS victim back to class". The Eugene Register-Guard. November 26, 1985.
[65] White, Ryan; Ann Marie Cunningham (1991). Ryan White: My Own Story. Dial Books. ISBN 978-0-8037-0977-5.
[66] Franklin, Tim (March 3, 1988). "Teen's Story of AIDS Prejudice Wins Hearts". The Chicago Tribune

who managed to help change the public perception of AIDS and increase public awareness that HIV/AIDS was not a gay-related immune deficiency and disease but a significant epidemic. [67]

Ryan was given just six more months to live when he received the AIDS diagnose but to the surprise of his doctors lived five more years than predicted. When Ryan White passed away one month before his high school graduation on April 8, 1990, his funeral was attended by 1,500 people including singers Michael Jackson and Elton John, football star Howie Long and Phil Donahue. Ronald Reagan wrote a tribute to Ryan that was published in the Washington Post after Reagan`s government had ignored AIDS for so long at the beginning of the crisis. [68]

Ryan White and his family rejected the term "Innocent Victim" because the phrase was often used at that time to imply that gay people were responsible for AIDS. Ryan`s mother stated later on that Ryan could never have lived that long as he did without the gay community and added that people in New York informed the family about the latest treatment options before they had known in Indiana. [69]

Fight for the Living – Care for the Dying

When the government permitted to sell the drug ACT to people who were suffering from AIDS, it wasn`t a cure but extended life for some people with AIDS. But people were still dying.

The AIDS units in hospitals were understaffed and overcrowded, and their staff was overworked and dealt with incredibly high rates of burnout and patients with weights of 90 pounds were waiting on wooden benches in hospital corridors

[67] Kokomo Mayor Swamped With Angry Calls Following Ryan White TV Movie". Associated Press. January 18, 1989
[68] 1,500 Say Goodbye to AIDS Victim Ryan White". Associated Press. April 11, 1990.
[69] https://www.nytimes.com/1992/09/24/garden/at-home-with-jeanne-white-ginder-a-son-s-aids-and-a-legacy.html

for a couple of hours. People with AIDS instead wanted to die at home than in those hospitals, and nobody thought that it was human for patients to suffer like that. Many activists believed that the least they could do was to give people a dignified death.

Back in the 80`s most hospitals were not prepared to respond to the AIDS crisis while paramedics were worried that gloves might not protect them from HIV. Some doctors assumed that at some point they had to breathe air from outside of the operating rooms since they were scared that they could breathe in the virus, which they believed subsequently attacked their lungs and infect them with HIV.

It is fair to say that there was plenty of stigmas out there even after the Center of Diseases Controls and Prevention made the announcement that HIV could only be transmitted through certain activities such as sexual activities and the shared use of needles or syringes.

People like Chris Brownlie strongly believed that it was essential to provide patients with AIDS with clean and warm places, where they could live out the last days of their existence and die without facing homelessness, overworked and stressed out doctors and nurses and relatives freaking out on them. People needed places where they could go to and be treated like human beings.

Hospice programs were already launched and running in cities such as New York City and San Francisco but not in many other parts of the States and the world. Chris Brownlie and his friends and fellow activists Michael Weinstein, Sharon Raphael, Mina Meyer, and others were part of the early AIDS hospice movement and co-founded the AIDS Hospice Foundation, which became the Aids Healthcare Foundation later on. Back in 1987, the group was heavily involved with the planning and negotiation of the Chris Brownlie Hospice on the grounds of the Barlow Respiratory Hospital.

Chris Brownlie was a hero and fighter and played a significant role when the Los Angeles County Board of Supervisors unexpectedly agreed to provide USD 2 million to AIDS care after an emotional plea for hospice care to the Los Angeles County Commission on AIDS and a protest and picketing of at the then-Supervisor's home.

The AHF had already believed back then that as human beings people should be committed to taking care of each other and subsequently opened the Chris Brownlie Hospice on December 26th, 1988, which was the county's first AIDS hospice and which provided 24/7-medical care to people living through the final stages of AIDS.

The openings of Carl Bean House followed in 1992 and Linn House in 1995, and all AHF hospices gave their patients the feeling that those were places where people actually helped, supported and were there for each other. AHF went on and opened new hospices in the Los Angeles area, and volunteers were invited to come in and roll up their sleeves, touch, hold and heal and support those who needed support.

Chris Brownlie was a passionate activist and one of the guiding forces in the AIDS movement in Los Angeles. His dedication to fight for the living and care for the dying confirms AHF's work and commitment until today. Chris Brownlie died at the age of 39 from AIDS at the Chris Brownlie Hospice on November 26, 1989.

By the time it ended its hospice operations in September 1996 the Chris Brownlie Hospice had provided more than 1,000 patients with a superior, specialized and compassionate final care at the end of their life. The AHF organization housed various departments in the building before the property was returned to the City of Los Angeles with a sunset memorial ceremony on January 26, 2013.[70]

---

[70] https://www.youtube.com/watch?v=p_2nqK2BoEs

Inspiration in the 1980s

When a young teenager grew up on a farm in Germany in the 1980s and felt that he was different, then there weren`t many things or people inspiring him to go out there and live his dreams. It also didn't help that I was the farmer`s oldest son and that both of my parents believed that it was my primary purpose and duty to step into the farmer`s footsteps and work on that farm day by day. And I started working when I was eight years old, and I was eight years old when I first experienced brutality through my old man`s hands, which ultimately ended my childhood.

It was hard, and there didn`t seem to be a way out back in the '80s until I finally embraced that being different wasn`t a bad thing at all which enabled me to believe in myself and my dreams, work hard and do whatever it takes. I think that one of the factors, which influenced me most was my passion for the performing arts, which I had felt from a very young age on.

And then there was the TV series Fame, which incorporated all of that and even if it aired in Germany for only 27 episodes still managed to inspire me. I absolutely credit Fame for my decision to join the theater group in school and overcome my fear of the bullies in middle and high school. Standing and performing on stage gave me that extra confidence to stand up for myself just like the Kids from Fame did.

I knew that the only way out was hard work and believing in myself and in those crazy dreams, which I had at that time and which took me to New York City almost twenty years later. And the fight for those dreams of mine started at home where both of my parents believed that farm work was more important than homework. I, however, felt that good grades could get me out of that farm and so I did my homework and studies in the nighttime after all the work on the farm was done. Fortunately, I had teachers in school, who inspired and believed in me. Some 30 years later I am still in contact with some of them and send them emails and Christmas cards from New York City, where I always wanted to be since I had been that young farm boy back in the

'80s and where the fictional New York City High School for the Performing Arts from Fame was based.

The American TV series Fame was produced between 1982 and 1987 and based on the 1980 movie of the same name. The series followed the lives of the drama, dance and music students and the lives of their teachers. Its popularity led to some hit records and live concert tours by the cast. Fame won several Emmy and Golden Globe Awards and was like a massive wave which fascinated millions of viewers worldwide and managed to inspire a new generation of performing artists until to this day. [71]

The four cast members from the original movie were Lee Curreri who played the shy musical genius, Bruno Martelli. Gene Anthony Ray played the tough hood kid Leroy Johnson from Harlem with a natural talent for dance, and who was the character I could most relate to. Albert Hague portrayed the German music teacher Benjamin Shorofsky, and the role of dance teacher Lydia Grant was played by Debbie Allen, who managed to maintain her high-profile career after the series ended. Ms. Allen also became the show's original choreographer, directed several episodes and co-produced one season. [72]

When I first watched Fame back in 1984, I could never have imagined that I would become a good friend with one of the cast members. I also would never have expected that I would meet most of the others, when I ended up standing and performing with the former Kids of Fame and my daughter Bella the theme song "Remember my name" on stage in Italy 33 years later at a reunion concert in 2017. "Remember my name" was Irene Cara's pop hit and first featured in the motion picture and was later on re-recorded and sung by cast member Erica Gimpel, who played Coco Hernandez in the TV series. [73] [74]

---

[71] Los Angeles Times: Archives – 'FAME,' NBC LEAD THE CRAFT EMMYS". Pqasb.pqarchiver.com. 1982-09-14. Retrieved 2012-10-03.

[72] https://www.youtube.com/watch?v=-XcvAFci6pw

[73] Roberts, David (2006). British Hit Singles & Albums (19th ed.). London: Guinness World Records Limited. p. 136. ISBN 1-904994-10-5.

[74] O'Connor, John J. (1983-03-03). "Tv – 'Kids From Fame,' Nbc Special". NYTimes.com. Retrieved 2012-10-03.

Back in the 80's Fame was part of my life for a short time. When it stopped airing in Germany, I had to get on with everything, which was going on at that time. I remember all those news reports about HIV and AIDS and I remember my father saying that the other farmers would lynch us if we brought AIDS to the village. I was very young when the AIDS crisis first started, but the topic of AIDS was something, which touched and affected me. It would take 15 years before the death of one of the cast members of Fame made me understand that I had to get involved in that fight myself.

But Fame had also opened another door back in the '80s, and that was my fascination for the performing arts and substantial interest and passion for the ballet. I grew up in a community whose members didn't have many dreams. Other farmer's sons believed that it was wrong to turn their back on their people and leave their parent's farms to fulfill their dreams at other places. But I felt inspired by the performing arts and all those fantastic things which their artists were standing for. Actors, dancers, and musicians seem to possess both the talent and passion for doing amazing and extraordinary things.

I was merely fascinated by the beauty and talent of those dancers, who worked so hard for their success and their dreams. Many of them lost their lives to AIDS. And just like other HIV infected celebrities such as Magic Johnson, Freddie Mercury, Liberace, Rock Hudson or Anthony Perkins they were the ones who gave AIDS a face in a time when a significant part of the population struggled to relate to the disease and sympathize with the ones who were suffering from AIDS.

Both their professional work, careers, and achievements but also their journeys still inspire millions of people until the current day. And therefore, I would like to take the opportunity to also remember those icons of dance in each of the sections in this book and will start with the incredible Michael Bennett and Alvin Ailey, whose stories ended in the 1980s and whose work still inspire many of us until to today.

Michael Bennett

I remember that pier dance in June 2008 when I was out with my friends on the pride weekend standing on that pier in Chelsea and awaiting the exceptional performance of one of the most popular and sought-after artists in that year, Ms. Jennifer Hudson. Portraying Effie White had been the acting debut of the former American Idol contestant and singer Jennifer Hudson, who ultimately received the Golden Globe Award and Academy Award for Best Supporting Actress for her role in "Dreamgirls" in the previous year. [75]

"Dreamgirls" was originally adapted from Michael Bennett`s 1981 Broadway musical of the same name. And even if all the eyes were on Jennifer Hudson on that night in June 2008 when she was performing her latest single "Spotlight" many of us still remembered the man, who had brought "Dreamgirls" to Broadway some 26 years earlier and before the AIDS epidemic hit the nation and took the lives of many talented artists including his own. [76]

Michael Bennett DiFiglia shared my birthday and was born on April 8th, 1943 in Buffalo New York and raised by an Italian American father and a Jewish mother. Bennett discovered his passion for the arts very early, studied dance and choreography in his teens and choreographed some shows in his high school before dropping out and accepting the role of Baby John in West Side Story and going on tour in the US and Europe. [77]

Bennett started working as a Broadway dancer in 1961 and after having appeared in several musicals became a featured dancer on the NBC pop music series Hullabaloo where he met fellow dancer and later-on wife, Donna McKechnie. Michael Bennett started working as a choreographer and "A Joyful Noise" in 1966 and "Henry, Sweet Henry" were followed by the hit musical "Promises, Promises" on Broadway in 1968, which ran

[75] https://en.wikipedia.org/wiki/Jennifer_Hudson
[76] https://www.ibdb.com/broadway-show/dreamgirls-3192
[77] Michael Bennett Biography (1943–)". Filmreference.com. Retrieved 2014-06-04.

for 1,281 performances and followed by "Twigs", "Company", "Follies", "Seesaw" and "Coco" with the incredible Katherine Hepburn. [78]

It is fair to say that "A Chorus Line" became one of Michael Bennett's biggest success. The musical was created based on hundreds of hours of taped sessions with Broadway dancers and co-choreographed and directed by Bennett and ultimately won nine Tony Awards and the 1976 Pulitzer Prize for Drama. When Michael picked up his award for best director for musical which was presented by Richard Burton, he said in his acceptance speech: "I really wanted this and so many people did so much to help me get this. But everybody that I have had the opportunity to work within the theater I mean they have taught me things and I only wanted one thing to be a Broadway director and I am and I wanted that one moment and I have it and I thank you." [79]

Bennett's next musical "Ballroom" was financially unsuccessful but still nominated for seven Tony Awards and Michael Bennett won one of them for Best Choreography. "A Chorus Line" was a tough act to follow, but "Dreamgirls" in 1981 became another huge success and I remember some of its music still being played at the world famous Roxy nightclub in New York some 25 years later. The musical was a backstage epic about a girl group like "The Supremes" and the expropriation of black music by a white recording industry. [80]

Michael Bennett always collaborated with his lifelong friend and assistant Bob Avian and he wasn't mainly known for a particular choreographic style but motivated by the form of the musical involved or the distinct characters interpreted. The song "One" from "A Chorus Line" for example reflects that the show is about professional dancers and shows the different phases of construction and rehearsal of the number being displayed with the last performance of the song-and-dance routine having all

---

[78] Promises, Promises" at the Internet Broadway Database, accessed November 14, 2008.
[79] https://www.youtube.com/watch?v=0iTqQ1fuUfM
[80] Mandelbaum, Ken (1990). A Chorus Line and the Musicals of Michael Bennett. St. Martins Press. ISBN 0-312-03061-4.

the gloss and polish being expected of a Broadway production. [81]

Michael Bennett had some affairs with both men and women and was known to be bisexual. He had a relationship with dancer, choreographer, and director Larry Fuller at the beginning of his life. He danced with Donna McKechnie in "Promises, Promises" and "Company" and created a role for her in "A Chorus Line," which won her a Tony Award for Best Actress in a Musical in 1976. They were married on December 4, 1976, but separated a few months later and consequently divorced in 1979. [82]

The then-wife of French Actor Jean-Pierre Cassel had an affair with Bennett in the late 1970s, and Sabine Cassel even left her family in Paris and followed Michael Bennett to New York before their relationship soured. [83]

Michael Bennett spent the final eight months of his time with his last lover Gene Pruitt and friend Bob Herr in Tucson, Arizona, where he received care at the Arizona Medical Center. Michael Bennett died from AIDS-related lymphoma at the age of 44 on July 2, 1987, and his memorial service took place at the Shubert Theater in New York City, which was the home of "A Chorus Line" at that time. He left a portion of his estate to fund research to fight the pandemic AIDS. [84]

Thirty-two years later I take my beautiful daughter Bella every Saturday morning to the Jacqueline Kennedy Onassis School of American Ballet Theater, which is based at 890 Broadway in the Flatiron District in New York. I wait for her outside of the studio and give her a big hug at the end of each

---

[81] Long, Robert Emmet (2001). Broadway, the Golden Years: Jerome Robbins and the Great Choreographer-directors: 1940 to the Present. Continuum International Publishing Group. ISBN 0-8264-1462-1

[82] Michael Bennett Biography (1943–)". Filmreference.com. Retrieved 2014-06-04

[83] Witchel, Alex. "A Long and Twisting Road Back to Broadway", The New York Times, March 24, 1996

[83] Kelly, Kevin (1990). One Singular Sensation: The Michael Bennett Story. New York: Doubleday. ISBN 0-385-26125-X

lesson. We walk along the long corridor and outside the other studios and watch the incredible and advanced students working hard and trying to become the best dancers they can be. We are surrounded by talent and ambition and we hear music, which was already played when Michael Bennett was still alive and living his dreams.

I just learned recently that Michael Bennett had purchased that same building on 890 Broadway in 1978 and converted it for the use as a rehearsal studio complex for dance and theater. Bennett sold the building in 1986, but it remains a rehearsal facility for American Ballet Theater and other dance companies. Michael Bennett spent a lot of time there and so do many other artists nowadays. His legacy lives on and he will never be forgotten. [85]

---

[85] https://www.nytimes.com/1986/11/02/theater/why-michael-bennett-has-said--goodbye-for-now-to-broadway.html?pagewanted=all

Alvin Ailey

My daughter Bella takes ballet lessons at the Jacqueline Kennedy Onassis School since September 2018, which is part of the American Ballet Theater. She loves ballet and most of us parents are very proud that our kid's art part of the ABT family. But it didn't start for us at that school on 890 Broadway when she was three years old. My little girl took her first steps in a dance school at the age of 2 when I signed her up for the Tiny Steps Program at the Ailey School. [86]

Bella first shared the joy of music and movement through rhythm and dance as her instructor Ms. Kay guided her and the other kids through fun and playful dance exercises. And when a trial class at JKO ended up in tears in May 2018, I took her back to the Ailey School on the very next day for a four weeks program so that she wouldn't lose her passion for the dance. Bella went straight back into it before joining JKO for its annual program in September 2018. Both of us loved the Ailey School, which was of course started by Alvin Ailey. [87]

Alvin Ailey was born by his 17 years-old-mother in Rogers, Texas on January 5th, 1931 and was only six years old, when his father walked out on him and his mother, who moved around often in the following years in order to find work during the Great Depression in a time when African Americans were experiencing racial segregation, violence, and lynching. [88]

Young Ailey grew up in a Southern Baptist Church with a fierce sense of black pride, which later on became a significant part of Ailey's signature works. He introduced himself as a choreographer and a black man whose roots were in the sun and the gospel church in the South where he grew up. Ailey believed until to the end that dance came from the people and should be returned to the people. [89]

---

[86] https://www.abt.org/training/dancer-training/

[87] https://www.theaileyschool.edu/programs/creative-movement/tiny-steps

[88] Dunning, Jennifer (1998). Alvin Ailey: A Life in Dance. New York: Da Capo Press. ISBN 9780306808258

[89] https://www.youtube.com/watch?v=44nqeAXLS-k

Alvin`s mother moved to Los Angeles in the fall of 1942, while Alvin stayed behind in Texas to finish his school year before he joined her by train at the age of 11. After he first attended a school in a primarily white school district where he felt out of place also because of his fear of whites the family moved to a predominantly black school district. As a teenager, Alvin Ailey sang, wrote poetry and showed a talent for languages and attended shows at the theater. [90]

Alvin Ailey became interested in dance when his school friend Carmen De Lavallade introduced him to Lester Horton`s Hollywood Studio, who became Alvin`s significant influence and mentor and provided him with both technique and a foundation. Horton`s school taught different dance styles and techniques including classical ballet, jazz, and Native-American dance and was the first multi-racial dance school in the States. [91]

Alvin Ailey had studied Roman Languages at different universities in California and decided to continue his studies in San Francisco in 1951 where he met Marguerite Johnson (Maya Angelou). They both performed a nightclub act called "Al and Rita," and Alvin also waited tables and danced at the New Orleans Champagne Supper Club before returning to study fulltime with Horton at the age of 22 at Southern California. Ailey`s dance studies focused on ballet and other forms of modern and ethnic dance but also art forms including painting, acting, music, set design and costuming. [92]

Alvin Ailey joined Horton`s company in 1953 and debuted in "Revue Le Bal Caribe." The company was left without an artistic director when Horton died in November of that same year. The company had outstanding contracts which required new work and when no else put himself forward, it was Alvin Ailey who stepped up and became the artistic director of the company at the age of 22 despite his lack of experience and young age. Alvin Ailey grew with the responsibility and choreographed, directed

---

[90] Judy Gitenstein, Alvin Ailey, New York: The Rosen Publishing Group, 2006.
[91] Dunning, Jennifer (1998). Alvin Ailey: A Life in Dance. New York: Da Capo Press. ISBN 9780306808258
[92] Judy Gitenstein, Alvin Ailey, New York: The Rosen Publishing Group, 2006

scenes and costume designs and ran rehearsals and also directed one of the shows for the company. [93]

Alvin Ailey and his friend Carmen De Lavallade moved to New York City in 1954 where he danced in the Broadway Shows "House of Flowers" by Truman Capote which starred Diahann Carroll, "Sing, Man, Sing" starring Harry Belafonte and "Jamaica" starring Ricardo Montalban. But Alvin Ailey was disappointed by the New Yorker modern dance scene in the '50s. When he failed to find a new mentor with a technique similar to Leslie Horton's he started to create works of his own and founded the Alvin Ailey American Dance Theater in 1958, which was inspired by the vision of Leslie Horton. [94]

One of the company's first pieces, "Blue Suite" was an instant success and defined Ailey's style. "Blues Suite" was derived from blues songs and expressed the pain and anger of many African American people and its choreography a mix of ballet, modern dance, jazz, and African dance techniques. Alvin Ailey pushed for a complete theatrical experience including costumes, lighting, and make-up. Alvin Ailey's signature work "Revelations" was based on "blood memories" of Texas and the blues, spirituals, and gospel, which resulted in the creation of his most popular and critically acclaimed work. [95]

79 of the company's more than 200 pieces were created by Alvin Ailey himself, who was very proud of running a multi-racial company after he had first wanted to give African American dancers, who were frequently excluded from performances by racist attitudes at that time the opportunity to dance and also address issues within the African American community. The company was one of the few exceptions who chose their dancers based solely on artistic talent and integrity. [96]

---

[93] Judy Gitenstein, Alvin Ailey, New York: The Rosen Publishing Group, 2006

[94] 9 LGBT People Of Color Who Changed History". LOGO News. Retrieved 2018-10-24

[95] Dunning, Jennifer (1996). Alvin Ailey: A Life In Dance. New York: Addison-Wesley Publishing Company, INC. ISBN 0-201-62607-1

[96] https://gaillardcenter.org/event/alvin-ailey-american-dance-theater

Alvin Ailey`s chorographical work for other companies includes "The River" by the American Ballet Theater in 1970 which brought together the finest dancers in the world with the leading role being danced by the only black dancer in the company. Ailey dedicated "Cry" to his beloved mother and black women everywhere, which turned out to be one of his biggest successes. [97]

A decade after the Alvin Ailey American Dance Theater was founded, which was constructed by Manhattan`s biggest construction company at that time Ailey founded the Alvin Ailey American Dance Center in 1969, which was renamed to the Ailey School in 1999. The school aimed to provide access to arts and dance to under-resourced communities and started with 125 students in Brooklyn and trains more than 3,500 dancers each year nowadays. The school moved its operations to Manhattan in 1970 and began to offer a Bachelor of Fine Arts Program in partnership with Fordham University in 1998. The Ailey School is still growing and well known to be the largest school for the training of committed dancers in New York City. [98]

The dancers who came to Ailey`s company came from different schools and had different backgrounds, from ballet to modern and jazz and hip-hop. Alvin Ailey didn`t train his dancers in a specific technique before they performed his choreography and instead requested his dancers to infuse his choreography with a personal style that best suited their talents, which brought classical dance into harmony with other forms of African-American expression including big band jazz. [99]

Alvin Ailey didn`t tell his mother about his dancing for the first two years. Ailey also maintained a largely closeted persona with regards to his sexuality, which came through his works; grandiose and lavish costume and set designs which were prevalent and appreciated by gay audiences and the display of glamorous masculinity and both female and male homosexuality

[97] https://www.rogallery.com/Ailey_Alvin/ailey-biography.html
[98] History & Philosophy". The Ailey School. 2016-03-02. Retrieved 2018-10-24
[99] 9 LGBT People Of Color Who Changed History". LOGO News. Retrieved 2018-10-24

and the acknowledgement of the sensual, intimate bond between men and women in dance in works he made for both the American Ballet Theater and his own company. [100]

Alvin Ailey wanted to spare his mother the social stigma of his AIDS/HIV death and requested his doctors to announce that he died of terminal blood dyscrasia. Alvin Ailey died from AIDS at the age of 58 on December 1st, 1989. Five thousand people showed up at his funeral to say good-bye. [101]

Ailey had already been awarded the Spingarn Medal from the NAACP in 1977 and the Kennedy Center Honors in 1988. Some 25 years after his death President Barack Obama selected Alvin Ailey to be posthumous recipient of the President Medal of Freedom. [102]

---

[100] Turnbaugh, Douglas Blair (2002). "Ailey, Alvin (1931–1989)" (PDF). glbtq: an encyclopedia of gay, lesbian, bisexual, transgender & queer culture. Archived from the original on December 30, 2008. Retrieved February 2, 2009

[101] Valerie Gladstone (October 23, 1996). "Frail, Strong and Dance Incarnate". The New York Times. Retrieved January 9, 2009

[102] President Obama Names Recipients of the Presidential Medal of Freedom". White House Office of the Press Secretary. November 10, 2014. Retrieved November 12, 2014

The end of the 1980s

The end of the '80s was marked by the tragic death of my grandfather, who had lost so much that his sad ending didn`t come as a surprise for many. I was just 15 years old when I took the call from the police who informed me about his death after the "farmer" had refused his father to return to the farm which he had once owned. Many believe that the "farmer`s" cold heart had pushed my grandfather into the sad decision to follow his wife and daughter into the afterlife, who had died under tragic circumstances before my birth.

Later on that evening I was on my own and alone on that farm since my parents and brother went to my aunt`s estate to inform her about the sad news. That night I made the decision that I would never become my old man`s victim and be pushed over the edge. I realized the damage that his actions had caused in other people`s life and promised myself that I would be remembered as a fighter and survivor one day. I was that skinny boy with glasses when things started to change after my grandfather`s death.

The inspiration through the power of the performing arts and being on stage in school had already provided me with confidence, but I started to develop the capability to fight back after that loss in my family. And I wanted to decide for myself what I wanted from life even if my parents had other plans for myself. I was sad about my grandfather`s passing, but I also realized that I could neither allow my parents nor the bullies in school to break me.

I finally started to stand up against the parents and others and made clear what I thought about them and their wrongdoings which was the first kind of activism I was involved with. I knew that I had to get on with things and take control. And that's what I did.

It was late on that summer night in 1989 when I washed my face and looked into the mirror of our bathroom. I took a deep breath and then I switched the light off when he switched the light on in his bathroom on the other side of the Atlantic. Josh Fenton had spent his morning on the beach of his parent's estate in the Hamptons playing softball with his friends, cracking jokes and having fun on another day of an epic summer in the Hamptons.

The American teenager and I were similar age but we could not have been more different. Josh was also the oldest son of his father and presumed heir to his family's fortune, but his childhood and teenage years were all about fun, a lot of fun. He was not just blessed with an existence full of privileges and parents who supported him but also with the perfect face and athletic body. Josh Fenton was a head turner and had everything going for him. He had all the opportunities and was able to live a life, which others were jealous of.

Josh and his sisters visited expensive private schools and he counted polo, tennis, and skiing to his hobbies. The family were regulars in St. Barth and owned a chalet in Aspen. There was no doubt that the convertible car would be waiting outside of the family's massive mansion on his 16th birthday. And Josh was popular; he was one of the most popular kids in his school and head of the polo and football teams. People described Josh as a winner and his family had connections which gave him access to all the opportunities as long as he wanted to take advantage of them.

When the handsome teenager looked into the mirror, he smiled for a moment. His skin was suntanned and he looked good. He had that sparkle in his eyes and considered himself as both blessed and lucky. But then there was this moment of insecurity which made him feel nervous. It was like a shadow and a dark thought on his mind, which started to become a regular unwanted guest in his life. And while both of us could indeed not have been more different, it was destiny and just a question of time, before our ways would cross in life and turn them upside down.

AIDS in the 1990s – The fighting back years

When I look back at the fight against HIV and AIDS and also at my own life then I realize that the '90s were all about taking control and fighting back. All my hard work in the 1980s paid off when I managed to step out of my parent`s shadow and accepted a job offer from a bank and was about to stand on my own feet at the age of 17. Banking wasn`t my first choice, but it felt like a relief when I left the years on the farm behind me and started working in our small town in August 1991.

There was so much going on in the world, and life felt suffocating after a while. Even my young colleagues were very conservative and saw themselves working in that bank for the next 45 years of their careers. But I just wanted to see more than that town and still had that big dream about New York City.

And so I left that small bank after completing my training and continued with a specialized high school in Cadenberge for another year in 1994. I was already very attached to the topic AIDS and delivered a presentation on the "The consequences of AIDS in Society" to my class and teacher Juergen Schwanemann, who I am still in contact with nowadays. That presentation was the first time that I was involved with the topic "AIDS" and explained to my classmates that there is no reason to treat people with the disease differently.

After leaving that school and my friends from Cadenberge, who I stayed connected with until to the current day I chose to work with the elderly for one year as an alternative to serving for ten months in the armed forces, which was obligatory in Germany at that time. When I started my studies at the University of Applied Science in Hanover, I was the first member of my German family to visit a university.

I was determined not to have to work for "the farmer" ever again and had plenty of jobs during my economic studies to support myself. I took on a part-time job in a bank and my good English language skills and looks helped me to score product presentation jobs at the international fairs and exhibitions, which Hanover was well known for. And despite all that work and socializing I managed to excel in my classes and became one of the hardest working students on campus.

The Fame TV series had vanished out of my life a long time ago, but I was driven and obsessed by the New York dream. And before my internships at Deutsche Bank in Frankfurt and Cologne in the following two years, I took a break in summer 1998 and traveled to the States to find out, if I wanted to live there. I was 24 years old when I arrived in New York City in July 1998. I was the new guy in town, and I was ready to make an impact. Little could I know that an encounter at the Roxy nightclub on 18th Street in Chelsea, New York City in that summer forever changed my existence.

AIDS had become the number one cause of death for men in the United States aged 25-44 years old in 1991 and by 1994 the leading cause of death for all Americans in that age group. The United Nations estimated that 16,000 people were newly infected with the virus every day and added that 30 million adults and children worldwide were infected with HIV. The CDC made the public aware that 49 percent of the AIDS-related deaths were accounted by African Americans in the States in 1998 and the AIDS World Health Organization announced at the end of the decade that HIV/AIDS had become the 4th biggest killer worldwide and that the AIDS epidemic was still growing. [103]

But the '90s were also defined by spreading awareness with health organizations, politicians, actors, athletes and musicians speaking up about HIV and AIDS. The red ribbon became the international symbol of AIDS awareness in 1991. Significant progress was made in preventing and testing with the FDA approving the female condom in 1993, an oral HIV test in 1994 and the first HIV home testing and collection kit in 1996. The number of new HIV and AIDS cases diagnosed in the States declined for the first time with the number of AIDS-related deaths in the States dropping by 47% by 1997 for reasons which will be

---

[103] https://www.hiv.gov/hiv-basics/overview/history/hiv-and-aids-timeline

further explained in this chapter. Drug resistance remained an area of grave concern in most of the '90s before life-saving discoveries were announced. [104] [105] [106] [107]

AIDS and the Clintons

When teenager Ryan White died of AIDS on April 8th, 1990 AIDS was no longer considered as a "gay disease." Four months after his death Congress enacted the Ryan White Comprehensive AIDS Resources Emergency (CARE) ACT in his honor, which became the United States' largest federally funded program providing funding for the care of low-income, uninsured and under-insured people living with HIV/AIDS and their families. [108]

The act remains an active piece of legislation until today and provides care for around 500,000 people a year and funds up to 2,567 organizations and local and state primary medical care providers, support services, healthcare provider and training programs. The extension of the act was signed by President Barack Obama when it was set to expire on September 30th, 2009. [109]

But how involved was President Bill Clinton with the fight against AIDS in the 1990s, when no president of the United States or his wife did much about the topic AIDS in the previous 12 years?

When the great movie star and close friend of the Reagans Rock Hudson was dying in 1985, no attempt was made by the White House to set a policy on the crisis, and it seemed instead

---

[104] https://visualaids.org/projects/the-red-ribbon-project
[105] https://www.healthline.com/health/celebrities-with-hiv#2
[106] https://www.hiv.gov/hiv-basics/overview/history/hiv-and-aids-timeline
[107] http://www.chicagotribune.com/news/ct-xpm-1998-10-07-9810080035-story.html
[108] Dirk Johnson (1990-04-09). "Ryan White Dies of AIDS at 18; His Struggle Helped Pierce Myths". The New York Times.
[109] The Ryan White HIV/AIDS Program". Health Resources and Services Administration, HHS.
Archived from the original on 2001-11-27. Retrieved 2007-09-11.

that its occupants were hoping that HIV/AIDS didn't exist or vanish from one day to the next one. Things were changing when Bill Clinton started to discuss AIDS in his campaign speeches and promised to implement the recommendations of the AIDS commission in its two reports which were gathering dust somewhere in the White House after they were presented to the previous 2 Republican Presidents Reagan and Bush Senior. [110]

Mr. Clinton suggested to broaden the HIV definition and include women and I.V. drug users and pushed for more research and development and treatment purposes. But did President Clinton keep his promises after all? Mr. Clinton achieved a lot during his years as a president and later on. He appointed a federal AIDS policy coordinator and tried unsuccessfully to lift the ban for HIV positive people on travel and immigration to the USA since Congress included the travel ban in a bill, he signed which included other priorities. [111] [112]

The funding for research, prevention, and treatment of AIDS increased by 39% since Bill Clinton became president and the Food and Drug Administration approved a new class of protease inhibitor drugs in 1996 under a new accelerated process for AIDS-related medications. Condoms were advocated for the first time by federal public service announcements and advisory groups, which distributed federal money and encouraged organizations to promote condoms. [113]

Clinton's health care reform proposal, which could have provided health coverage for all Americans living with HIV was rejected by Congress, but Clinton managed to have the Ryan White Care Act to be fully funded. The act was supposed to provide $275 million to cities for AIDS treatment and ended being

---

[110] http://yastreblyansky.blogspot.com/2016/03/does-anybody-remember-clintons-and-aids.html
[111] https://www.nytimes.com/1992/03/28/us/1992-campaign-verbatim-heckler-stirs-clinton-anger-excerpts-exchange.html
[112] http://yastreblyansky.blogspot.com/2016/03/does-anybody-remember-clintons-and-aids.html
[113] http://community.seattletimes.nwsource.com/archive/?date=19960818&slug=2344764

funded at $738.5 million in 1996 and up 117 percent over his first three years. [114]

Congress denied Clinton's request to provide drug treatment on demand to stop the spread of HIV by intravenous drug users. The President, however, created an office of alternative medicines at the National Institutes of Health and encouraged States to fund such treatments under Medicaid coverage. Under Bill Clinton's leadership the Center for Disease Control and Prevention's budget expanded confidential and anonymous testing for HIV or AIDS as well AIDS counseling was offered in 900 testing sites and the Kennedy-Kassebaum bill prohibited health plans from providing lower coverage for AIDS than other life-threatening illnesses. [115] [116]

The government in the States was significantly influenced by other countries, and AIDS workers welcomed French President Jacques Chirac addressing Africa's top AIDS conference on December 7th, 1997 when he asked the world's wealthiest nations to create an AIDS therapy support fund to increase the number of AIDS studies and experiments and help people in Africa. Africa struggled to provide care for two-thirds of the world's patients with AIDS without having access to expensive AIDS therapies. [117]

The French president's message wasn't forgotten. The International Human Rights Day/Treatment Action Campaign (TAC) was consequently launched on December 10th, 1998 to campaign for all South Africans to have better access to HIV treatments by raising public awareness and understanding about issues surrounding the availability and affordability use of HIV treatments. People no longer wanted to accept AIDS as a death sentence as the disease was described back in the 1980s. [118]

---

[114] http://community.seattletimes.nwsource.com/archive/?date=19960818&slug=2344764

[115] http://yastreblyansky.blogspot.com/2016/03/does-anybody-remember-clintons-and-aids.html

[116] http://community.seattletimes.nwsource.com/archive/?date=19960818&slug=2344764

[117] https://www.revolvy.com/topic/Timeline%20of%20HIV/AIDS

[118] https://tac.org.za/news/where-are-our-rights-this-international-human-rights-day/

Bill Clinton made the clear decision to be heavily involved with the fight against HIV/AIDS in Africa and his administration implemented a $325million "Leadership and Investment in Fighting an Epidemic Initiative to fight AIDS around the world" in 1999 which focused on 15 target countries, including 14 in Sub-Saharan Africa plus India, which was the country with the highest numbers of new infections and severe epidemics at that time. [119]

Clinton`s vice president Gore was the chair of meetings of the United Nations Security Council on HIV/AIDS in Africa in January 2000, which was the first time that the council addressed the epidemic. The president signed the Global AIDS and Tuberculosis Relief Act of 2000, which authorizes a U.S. contribution of $ 150 million, which made the country to the most significant bilateral donor of HIV/AIDS assistance for the prevention, care, and education and funding of other projects in this area in Africa and in the world. And later on Bill Clinton`s wife Senator Hillary Clinton fought against a significant loss of funding for New York and many other states during a Senate debate over the reauthorization of the Ryan White Care Act which resulted with Hillary Clinton`s leadership on this issue being praised. [120]

Bill and Hillary Clinton`s engagement during the fight against HIV/AIDS was mirrored when the couple viewed the AIDS quilt, which was on display in the National Mall in Washington in 1996. The president told a reporter "I remember when Hillary and I walked on the Mall to see the AIDS Quilt. We walked back and forth to see all the squares, and we were looking for people's names we knew. We had several people that we`d known and cared about who had had HIV, and it had grown into AIDS, and they had not survived it. It was a personally emotional thing, seeing the love and devotion that those sections of the quilt represented for all those people who died prematurely, and knowing that now, with medicine, they didn`t have to die anymore, if we did the right things. It was a very emotional day." [121]

---

[119] https://2001-2009.state.gov/r/pa/ho/pubs/8531.htm
[120] https://2001-2009.state.gov/r/pa/ho/pubs/8531.htm
[121] https://www.pbs.org/wgbh/pages/frontline/aids/interviews/clinton.html

Hoping for Miracles - The AIDS Cocktail

Public pressure grew and when NBA star Magic Johnson announced on November 7th, 1991 that he is HIV positive and it became evident for many people that everyone could catch the HIV. While in the early 1980s most AIDS cases occurred among whites, the cases among African Americans, Hispanics, Asians/Pacific Islanders, and American Indians/Alaska Natives increased steadily and by 1996 more cases occurred in the African American community than in any other population. [122]

Back in the 1980s, it was well established that one single drug cannot fight HIV and scientists were hoping that they could win the fight against AIDS if patients had the choice between different classes of HIV medications, which were designed to block the HIV virus at specific points in its life cycle. They were dreaming and hoping that the combination of drugs lowers the virus's ability to reproduce, infect and ultimately kill the patient and enable HIV patients to live long and relatively healthy lives as long as they take their medication.

But people wanted to know what was happening behind the walls of pharmaceutical companies and research institutes after the rise and fall of AZT in the 1980s. Billions of dollars had been spent and 15 years of undivided attention of some of the most intelligent people in the world had failed to deliver a cure at that stage. AIDS had already killed almost 6 million people when scientists were finally getting excited about a possible treatment for HIV/AIDS at the 11th International Conference on AIDS in Vancouver in Canada in July 1996 when news got out about a drug cocktail that may drastically reduce the level of HIV in the blood and even stop the virus from replicating. [123]

Doctors and patients in the developed world who were most likely be the only ones benefiting from the expensive new drug therapy were raising the question if the drug cocktail provided

---

[122] https://www.cdc.gov/mmwr/preview/mmwrhtml/mm5021a2.htm
[123] https://www.independent.co.uk/news/cocktail-opens-new-chapter-on-aids-1328432.html

symptoms free life and be able to control the HIV in the long term. People were hopeful because this time the high-profile launch of the new drugs used in the cocktail was supported by a preliminary study from the Aaron Diamond Aids Research Center in New York. The study involved 12 gay men with an average age of 34 who had all become infected with HIV within three months before the trial which had given the virus little time to mutate. [124]

None of the patients had received previous treatments before they were given the cocktail which consisted of AZT and 3TC both produced by Glaxo-Wellcome as well as Norvir, which was a new class of drug. Norvir was classified as a protease inhibitor and just became available six months ago. Norvir was offered by Abbott Laboratories, and the expectation was that the protease inhibitor blocked an enzyme crucial to the multiplication of the HIV Virus and that AZT and 3TZ (reverse transcriptase inhibitors) worked at an earlier stage, which delivered the virus a "one-two" punch. [125]

Nine months after the treatment had started the HIV levels in nine of the twelve men had fallen to below the level of detection, and the white blood cell counts risen significantly. Back in 1996 it was not clear if the replication of the virus was halted after the drug treatments were stopped, which was an ethical problem for the scientists, who already expected back then that the virus was hiding in other parts of the body such as the nervous systems, when it wasn't detectable in the blood anymore.

Scientists were already worried that the HIV strains emerging became resistant to all drugs in the cocktail and that stopping the treatment could produce a rebound effect and accelerated replication of the virus with devastating results. Back in 1996 many scientists seriously questioned that the triple therapy approach was a cure for HIV and AIDS, but it was

[124] https://www.independent.co.uk/news/cocktail-opens-new-chapter-on-aids-1328432.html
[125] https://www.independent.co.uk/news/cocktail-opens-new-chapter-on-aids-1328432.html

understood as an experiment which had knocked out that HIV and people were hoping that it could kill the virus over an extended period. [126]

People were excited, but also aware that longer studies over a period of one to two years involving a higher number of HIV positive patients were necessary to determine, if the drugs cocktail was the ultimate solution.

The Lazarus Effect

By summer 1999 many AIDS patients who had signed up for the triple therapy experienced the Lazarus effect and raised like the biblical figure from the dead. And even if AIDS still infected about 40,000 new people every year in the United States, the actual death rate had dropped drastically. It seemed that the previously automatic death sentence AIDS had become a chronic but quite often manageable disease. One of its sufferers who experienced the so-called Lazarus effect was the Wisconsin woman Beth Bye, who stated in spring 1996 that she had returned from the dead. [127]

Okay, Ms. Bye hadn`t died, but death seemed near with her body being ravaged in the late stages of the AIDS infection and she had AIDS-related dementia and blindness. Beth made funeral arrangements and considered moving into a hospice for her remaining days when medical science offered her another option in the form of the drug cocktail. Within two months of beginning the triple cocktail treatment which is also known as Highly Active Antiretroviral Therapy (HAART) Ms. Bye`s viral load - a measure of new AIDS virus produced in the body – dropped to undetectable levels with her red and white blood cell counts normalizing and her immune system working again. Like many others, Ms. Bye was able to walk long distances again and

---

[126] https://www.independent.co.uk/news/cocktail-opens-new-chapter-on-aids-1328432.html

[127] https://aidsinfo.nih.gov/news/493/attacking-aids-with-a-cocktail-therapy--drug-combo-sends-deaths-plummeting

eventually even returned to work and a relatively healthy and productive life.

Many credited the HAART therapy, which disrupts HIV at different stages in its replication, for one of the reasons why the domestic AIDS death rate dropped by 47 percent in 1997 in connection with increased access to care, growing expertise, and experience in caring for HIV-infected patients and the decrease of new HIV infections in the late 1980`s due to prevention efforts. [128]

The HAART Therapy still had its drawbacks in 1999 and never became a cure for AIDS. And even if the virus became undetectable in the blood, it was still hiding in other parts of the body as suggested three years earlier. And the belief that the virus could not be transmitted due to lower viral loads led to a lapse in certain prevention practices with HIV being spread.

The combination therapy was also expensive and required a complicated treatment regimen. Its patients had to follow a strict dosing schedule to avoid that the protease inhibitors could result in the emergence of HIV strains that are resistant to treatment. Furthermore, studies had already shown that the viral load could rapidly rebound to high levels if patients decide to discontinue a part or all of the triple therapy. Additionally, AIDS treatments could interact with other commonly prescribed drugs, which led to increased levels in the blood.

Other possible side effects at that time were that the therapy could start or worsen existing diabetes or high blood sugar. Some patients were also experiencing a type of weight redistribution with face and limbs becoming thin and breasts, stomach or neck enlarging. Researchers were worried about the possible long-term effects for patients due to the possibility of high cholesterol levels for some patients, which could increase

---

[128] https://aidsinfo.nih.gov/news/493/attacking-aids-with-a-cocktail-therapy--drug-combo-sends-deaths-plummeting

the risk for cardiovascular complications such as strokes and heart attacks. [129]

Pregnant women and Children

I do have a healthy daughter who is very active and has many interests, and like other expecting parents, I was relieved when I learned at the beginning of the second trimester of the pregnancy that my baby was healthy. But many babies became infected with HIV through their mothers near the time of birth during the AIDS crisis before pregnant women were given the opportunity to take AZT and other HIV drugs after the first trimester of their pregnancy to decrease the risk of their babies being born with HIV by more than 66%. [130]

The Public Health Service Task Force highly recommended in 1998 to delay the therapy until after the 10th or 12th week of pregnancy after the fetus's organs have gone through the most rapid development. The risk of adverse effects of AZT on fetal development had to be balanced with the mother's health and possible transmission of HIV to the fetus.

Further guidelines recommended treating HIV infected children younger than one year and all HIV infected children of any age with symptoms of HIV and their immune systems being attacked with anti-HIV drugs. It was further strongly suggested to defer the drug's therapy for HIV-infected children with no signs and the risk of the disease being considered as low depending on their viral load and immune status. [131]

AIDS death rates had dropped significantly by the end of the 1990s and scientists were optimistic that they would overcome many more hurdles in the new millennium and hoped that it could

---

[129] https://aidsinfo.nih.gov/news/493/attacking-aids-with-a-cocktail-therapy--drug-combo-sends-deaths-plummeting
[130] https://aidsinfo.nih.gov/news/493/attacking-aids-with-a-cocktail-therapy--drug-combo-sends-deaths-plummeting
[131] https://aidsinfo.nih.gov/news/493/attacking-aids-with-a-cocktail-therapy--drug-combo-sends-deaths-plummeting

be possible to eventually create an AIDS preventive vaccine and new therapies, which would effectively treat patients when drug-resistant strains of HIV develop. But scientists were also aware that what humankind really needed were drugs which could wipe out AIDS sometime shortly and which didn't exist at that time. [132]

And many pharmaceutical companies were dreaming and hoping to develop a potent, inexpensive, easy to administer and relatively nontoxic even after prolonged periods drug, which could be active against viral strains which were resistant to currently available drugs. People were both wondering and praying if the new millennium would bring that perfect drug.

AIDS Healthcare Foundation

After the Aids Hospice Foundation had opened the hospices in California in the 1980's they noticed a few years later that the drugs and treatments for HIV infections were working and that the life expectancies of HIV patients were extending. When the drug cocktail became available, the AHF decided to offer it to patients in its 3 25 bed hospices who were close to death to see, if it could help them. The results were astonishing when AIDS patients who had been almost dead one year ago and whose bodies had been covered by skin cancer gained 20 lbs with the cancer being gone.

It was the first time that treatment outpaced the HIV virus. But since a government program wasn't set up at that time and the government didn't cover the costs for drugs for people who couldn't afford them the AHF was providing those drugs without getting reimbursements not only in the hospices but also in the clinic, which brought the organization close to bankruptcy. But the organization couldn't let people die who could be saved, and virtually all of their patients got better within 1 or 2 months and returned to their life before hardly anybody had left the hospices.

---

[132] https://aidsinfo.nih.gov/news/493/attacking-aids-with-a-cocktail-therapy--drug-combo-sends-deaths-plummeting

The AHF realized that what patients needed were medical treatments in outpatient centers and made the move to change the name of the organization to AIDS Healthcare Foundation to respond to an overcrowding health system for HIV patients and open new clinics. The new mission of the AHF was to be there for their patients in every step on the way and not just in their final days.

AHF launched a health care program for HIV positive patients so that they were on a plan which addressed their specific needs and not get left behind and lost in one of the regular health maintenance organizations. The organization started to open clinics for women and minorities to take their specific needs into account, and patients felt save and were surrounded by professionals, who knew what they were doing and who cared for them.

To grow as an organization and fund their mission, the Aids Healthcare Foundation chose to create its own business as a non-profit organization to generate revenues for its open operations and entered into a social enterprise model. The AHF's business plan included the opening of their pharmacies and Out of Closet clothes stores, which eventually grew into the largest HIV related retail business.

The AHF kept growing and operated by 1999 6 outpatient clinics in LA country and 15 Out of the Closet stores. The organization was well known for being an advocate for people living with HIV or AIDS and began to expand and contracted with Florida to provide care in all 67 counties. Magic Johnson launched a free HIV clinic in Miami Beach, and four other Magic Johnson Clinics were opened across the country in collaboration with AIDS Healthcare Foundation.

The AHF didn't expect people to come to them; the AHF traveled to them instead and went to places such as Mississippi were the stigma was intense and the need so big. Later on, the AHF went on an HIV testing tour across the country, which was part of a three weeks testing campaign to increase the number of Americans being tested for HIV. In order to reach as many people as possible in times before the internet was available to almost everyone HIV testing vans were driven across the United States and shops were set up in parking launches and next to nightclubs and other popular venues with the tour starting in the West Adams district and ending in Washington DC on National HIV Testing Day on June 27th, 1999. [133]

---

[133] https://www.youtube.com/watch?v=p_2nqK2BoEs&t=4s

Rudolf Nureyev

People remember Rudolf Nureyev as the Lord of Dance and as an artist with incredible talent and personality, who came out and grasped the audience and held it like in a love affair. Follow dancers described Nureyev as a blazing star, a meteor, who inspired a whole generation of dancers all over the world and future generations to come. Sex appeal, mesmerizing on and off stage made him one of the 20th century most charismatic figures who was adored by millions. Rudolf Nureyev dominated the world of ballet for more than 30 years through his beauty, passion and his affection to the West in the height of the cold war. Nureyev`s wild lust for life always fostered a romantic image that lasted until his end. [134] [135]

The man who would be widely regarded as the greatest male ballet dancer of his generation was born as Rudolf Khametovich Nureyev on a crowded Trans-Siberian train near Siberia, the Soviet Union on March 17th, 1938 and experienced very humble beginnings and a childhood, which was defined by a grim property. His early years were hard and Rudolf Nureyev remembered often of going hungry in his childhood. [136]

Rudolf Nureyev fell in love with dance when his mother took him and his three older sisters to the ballet "Song of the Cranes" for the first time when he was six years old, which changed his childhood. Nureyev saw the ballet "Swan Lake" in the following year and knew instantly that this was what he wanted to do for a living. On the next morning Rudolf was dancing away in one of the rooms in the Kindergarten and was encouraged to participate in Bashkir folk performance where his teachers noticed his talent and suggested to him to start training in St. Petersburg. [137] [138]

[134] https://www.youtube.com/watch?v=iFXgou31qHw
[135] Lord of the dance - Rudolf Nureyev at the National Film Theatre, London, 1–31 January 2003 , by John Percival, The Independent, 26 December 2002
[136] https://www.youtube.com/watch?v=iFXgou31qHw
[137] "Rudolf Nureyev Foundation official website". www.nureyev.org.
[138] RUDOLF NUREYEV - BIOGRAPHY - 3 YEARS IN THE KIROV THEATRE, Rudolf Nureyev Foundation official website.

But Nureyev had overcome several hurdles and concealed his passion for the dance from his father, who wanted him to follow him to the army. Furthermore, he wasn't able to enroll in a major ballet school until 1955 when he was 17 years old due to the disruption of cultural life in his country after the Second World War. But Nureyev persisted, and the ballet master of the Vaganova Academy of Russian Ballet of Saint Petersburg Alexander Pushkin and his wife allowed Nureyev to live with them after the ballet school accepted him. [139] [140]

Other dancers who became principal dancers in their careers entered the training at the Vaganova Ballet Academy at the age of 9 and stayed for the entire program of 9 years while Nureyev ended up staying for only three years. [141]

It is believed that despite his late arrival at the age of 17 he absorbed so much from Puskin that he probably gained more out of his relatively short time as a student and as a dancer than many other artists there could have gained in twice the time. Nureyev was aware that he had to make up for three to five years in ballet education at a ballet school and was required to acquire the maximum of technical skills within a short time, which enabled him to become the best dancer working on perfection during his whole career. [142] [143]

At the end of his course, he went to a competition in Moscow and amazed everybody with the way he danced, which led to his acceptance by the Kirov Ballet (nowadays Mariinsky) where he moved immediately beyond the corps level and performed in solo roles as a principal dancer from the outset. [144]

Rudolf Nureyev danced in 15 parts from 1958 to 1961 and became one of Soviet Union's best-known dancers before he

---

[139] https://www.youtube.com/watch?v=iFXgou31qHw
[140] John Bridcut (2007). Nureyev: From Russia With Love (Motion picture). BBC.
[141] https://www.youtube.com/watch?v=iFXgou31qHw
[142] https://www.youtube.com/watch?v=iFXgou31qHw
[143] Mikhail Baryshnikov was a pupil of the Vaganova Ballet Academy from 1964 to 1967.
[144] Rudolf Nureyev, Charismatic Dancer Who Gave Fire to Ballet's Image, Dies at 54, by Jack Anderson, The Independent, 7 January 1993.

was allowed to leave the country and dance in Vienna at the International Youth Festival. The Minister of Culture informed him afterward that he would not be allowed to travel abroad again, which didn't hold him back from interrupting a performance of Don Quixote for 40 minutes and insisting on dancing in tights and not in the customary trousers, which was adopted in performances later on. [145]

When the ballet company was planning to go on a tour to Paris and London, it was unlikely that the sensation in the Soviet Union with a rebellious character and non-conformist attitude was allowed to go on the trip to the West, which was of crucial importance to the country's ambition to portray its cultural supremacy. But when French representatives of the organizers of the tour saw Nureyev dancing in Leningrad, they urged the authorities to let him dance in Paris. [146]

Nureyev was allowed to go to Paris, where his performances electrified audiences and critics. But the ballet company's management and the KGB were aware that he was mingling with foreigners and frequently visited gay bars in Paris and enjoyed that new found freedom. The KGB was getting nervous and wanted to send him back to the Soviet Union. When the dance company gathered at the Le Bourget Airport to fly to London Nureyev was told that he had to return to Moscow for a special performance in the Kremlin on June 16th, 1961. [147]

Nureyev became suspicious and expected to be imprisoned as soon as he returned to the Soviet Union when he was told after his initial refusal to leave for Moscow that his mother had fallen severely ill. Nureyev managed to get away from the KGB minders with the help from French police and the Parisian socialite friend Clara Saint, who was engaged to the son of the French Minister of Culture Andre Malraux. [148]

[145] https://www.youtube.com/watch?v=iFXgou31qHw
[146] John Bridcut (2007). Nureyev: From Russia With Love (Motion picture). BBC.
[147] Watson, P., Nureyev: A Biography, p.151
[148] "The girl who led Nureyev to defect". The Australian. 14 December 2015.

Nureyev decided to ask for asylum and chose to stay in Paris, which was the first defection of a Soviet artist during the Cold War and which created an international sensation. The Soviet authorities, later on, forced his parents and former dance teacher Pushkin to write letters and urge him to return without effect.

When Rudolf Nureyev petitioned the Soviet government in later years to be allowed to visit his mother, he was refused to do so until 1987 when his mother was dying, and Mikhail Gorbachev consented to the visit who also supported the reunion of West and East Germany in 1989. When Rudolf Nureyev was invited to dance the role of James in LaSylphide with the Mariinsky Ballet at the Mariinsky Theatre in St. Petersburg in 1989, he was given the opportunity to see many of his former teachers and colleagues who he hadn`t seen since his defection 28 years earlier. [149]

Back in summer 1961 Rudolf Nureyev was signed up by the Grand Ballet du Marquis de Cuevas within a week after his defection and performed in "The Sleeping Beauty" before Rudolf Nureyev was offered a contract to join the Royal Ballet in the United Kingdom as a principal dancer. The Russian dancer appeared and partnered with the Prima Ballerina Dame Margot Fonteyn in Giselle on February 21st, 1962 after Nureyev first appeared in the United Kingdom at a ballet matinee organized by Fonteyn in 1961. [150]

Rudolf Nureyev and Margot Fonteyn became long-standing dance partners, and Nureyev once said that they danced with one body and one soul. Later on, he celebrated long-standing dance partnerships with Yvette Chauvire of the Paris Opera Ballet, with Eva Evdokimova who he appeared together with in La Sylphide in 1971 and the Sleeping Beauty in 1975 and with

[149] https://www.youtube.com/watch?v=iFXgou31qHw
[150] Acocella, Joan (October 8, 2007). "Wild Thing; Rudolf Nureyev, onstage and off". The New Yorker. Retrieved 2018-09-30.

Sonia Arova at New York City`s Brooklyn Academy of Music during his debut on a stage in America in 1962. [151] [152]

The challenge for other dancers working with that master of perfection was to follow suit, share Nureyev`s total commitment for dance, surpassing oneself and stepping on that kind of high-speed train. Nureyev was well known to be an unusual man in all respects and respected for his instinctive, intelligence, constant curiosity and extraordinary discipline and his love for performing. [153]

He stayed with the Royal Ballet until 1970 and was promoted to Principal Guest Artist, which enabled him to focus on his increasing schedule of international guest appearances and tours. He continued to perform regularly with the Royal Ballet until he committed his future to the Paris Opera Ballet in the 1980s. [154]

The artist without a country became a naturalized citizen of Austria in 1982 and was appointed as director of the Paris Opera Ballet in 1983, where he directed and continued to dance to promote younger dancers. Nureyev became a master of classical techniques and a model for an entire generation of dancers. Many believe that the standards of male dancing having risen so visibly in the West after the 1960s was mainly because of his inspiration. [155] [156]

Male roles received much more choreography in his productions of the classics than in other choreographer`s productions, and he crossed borders between the classical ballet and modern dance by performing both. Nureyev excelled in modern and classical dance and was the originator before many

[151] Rockwell, John (13 January 1993). *"Rudolf Nureyev Eulogized And Buried in Paris Suburb – via NYTimes.com.*
[152] https://www.youtube.com/watch?v=iFXgou31qHw
[152] https://www.youtube.com/watch?v=iFXgou31qHw
[153] Watson, P., Nureyev: A Biography
[154] 1961 - Nureyev defects to the West". Retrieved 24 March 2014.
[155] https://www.youtube.com/watch?v=iFXgou31qHw
[155] https://en.wikipedia.org/wiki/Rudolf_Nureyev#cite_note-29
[156] Sir John Tooley - Nureyev's influence on the development of Ballet in the West, official site of the Nureyev foundation.

dancers nowadays receive training in both the classical ballet and modern dance. His work lived on when several principals at the Paris Opera Ballet under his direction became ballet directors themselves and continued Nureyev`s ideas at major ballet companies such as the Vienna State Ballet, the Stanislavski Theatre of Moscow and the Grand Theatre of Bordeaux. [157] [158]

Nureyev remained a dancer and chief choreographer at the Paris Opera Ballet until 1989, and his artistic directorship lifted the company out of a dark period. He worked tirelessly, staged new versions of classical ballets and commissioned some of the most groundbreaking works at that time. The productions of some of his interpretations of numerous artistic works such as Romeo and Juliet became popular successes. When he was sick towards the end of his life, he worked on a final production of La Bayadere which closely followed the Mariinsky Ballet version which he had danced as a young man. [159]

Rudolf Nureyev was a perfectionist and didn't have much patience with rules, limitations, hierarchical order and sometimes with the failings of others interfering with his work. He socialized with Freddie Mercury, Jackie Kennedy Onassis, Mick Jagger, Liza Minelli, Andy Warhol, and Lee Radziwill and was a regular guest at the legendary New Yorker discotheque Studio 54 in the late 1970s until he developed an intolerance for celebrities. [160]

At the same Rudolf Nureyev was considered to be a loyal and generous friend in and out of the world of the ballet for decades. Most of the ballerinas who danced with Nureyev remembered that he was a very considerate partner and helped

---

[157] https://www.youtube.com/watch?v=iFXgou31qHw
[157] https://www.youtube.com/watch?v=iFXgou31qHw

them during difficult times when they had trouble finding roles. [161]

Rudolf Nureyev was either described as bisexual, because of his heterosexual relationships as a younger man, or gay. There were rumors about Nureyev`s rather exciting affairs and relationships including numerous bathhouse visits and anonymous pickups. [162]

It changed his life when he met the soloist at the Royal Danish Ballet Erik Bruhn while on tour in Denmark. Erik Bruhn became his lover, closest friend, and protector. Nureyev had admired the Danish dancer for years and seen filmed performances of him while Bruhn was on tour in the Soviet Union with the American Ballet Theater before the two dancers met in Denmark. They were stylistically very different, but became a couple and remained together on and off and had a very volatile relationship for 25 years until Erik Bruhn`s death in 1986. [163]

The other love in his life was the 23-year-old American dancer and classical arts student Robert Tracy, who Rudolf Nureyev met in 1973 and had a two-and-a-half-year love affair with. Robert Tracy became Nureyev`s secretary and companion for over 14 years in an open relationship. Tracy stated that Nureyev had relationships with three women and had always wanted a son and once planned to father one with actress Nastassja Kinski. [164] [165]

Rudolf Nureyev`s was an artist, who worked and worked and worked. No other male dancer had such a long-lasting career than him, and he continued to perform until the late 1980s. Rudolf Nureyev refused to let AIDS held him back as an artist after he was tested HIV positive in 1984. Rudolf Nureyev simply

[161] Watson, P., Nureyev: A Biography, p.321

[162] Bentley, Toni (2 December 2007). "Nureyev: The Life - Julie Kavanagh - Book Review. The New York Times.

[163] Acocella, Joan (October 8, 2007). "Wild Thing; Rudolf Nureyev, onstage and off". The New Yorker. Retrieved 2018-09-30.

[164] Nureyev and me, and interview with Robert Tracy, by John Ezard and CarolynSoutar,2003,TheGuardian,NYC

[165] Ezard, John; Soutar, Carolyn (30 January 2003). "Nureyev and me". The Guardian.

denied that anything was wrong with his health. Nureyev`s health began to decline only in summer 1991, and he entered the final phase of the disease in spring 1992. At that time Nureyev appeared as a conductor in front of the audience at Musa Caeli Tatar Academic Opera and Ballet Theater in Kazan in March 1992 and returned to Paris with a high fever and was admitted to a hospital in the suburb northwest of Paris, where he was operated. [166]

His main inspiration to fight the disease was an invitation to conduct Romeo and Julia at a benefit at the American Ballet Theater at the Metropolitan House in New York on May 6th, 1992, where he was elated at the reception. [167]

Rudolf Nureyev`s last public appearance took place on October 8th, 1992 at the premiere at Palais Garnier of the new production of La Bayadere that he choreographed for the Paris Opera, which was based on a photocopy of the original score by Minkus which he had managed to obtain when in Russia in 1989. It became a personal triumph and his way to say goodbye when his condition was evident. After the premiere the cast gathered on stage to salute to the man who had dedicated his life to their art and the French government honored his genius when the French Culture Minister Jack Lang presented Nureyev with France`s highest cultural award, the Commandeur de l`Ordre des Arts et des Lettres. [168] [169]

Rudolf Nureyev re-entered the hospital in Levallois-Perret on November 20th, 1991 and remained there until to the end. Rudolf Nureyev died of the complications of AIDS at the age of 54 on January 6th, 1993. His funeral was held in the marble foyer of the Paris Garnier Opera House, and many paid tributes to his brilliance as a dancer. Oleg Vinogradov from the Mariinsky Ballet in Saint Petersburg stated that what Nureyev did in the West, he

[166] https://www.youtube.com/watch?v=iFXgou31qHw
[167] Nureyev Did Have AIDS, His Doctor Confirms". *The New York Times*. John Rockwell. 16 January 1993. Retrieved 18 September 2011.
[168] Watson, P., *Nureyev: A Biography*, p.441
[169] https://www.youtube.com/watch?v=iFXgou31qHw

could never have done in Russia and when his coffin was lowered into the ground music from the last act of Giselle was played, and his ballet shoes were cast into the grave along with white lilies. [170]

Nureyev`s influence on the ballet over 50 years had been incredible, and Nureyev went into history as one of the leading figures in his generation. His reputation in Russia was restored when his name was reentered in the history of the Mariinsky, and some of his items were displayed at the theatre museum in Saint Petersburg after he had been denied a place in the Mariinsky Ballet history for all those years and the famous Vaganova Academy named a rehearsal room in his honor. [171]

The Centre National de Costume de Scene has a permanent collection of Rudolf Nureyev`s costumes since October 2013, and he was inducted into the Legacy Walk in 2015. My daughter Bella and I will visit his grave and the exhibition at the Centre National de Costume de Scene during our next visit in Paris in July 2019 and remember the most likely greatest ballet dancer of all times in our way. [172]

The Paris Opera decided to organize a dance night to remember Nureyev every ten years since he died in 1993. The first two dance nights were scheduled on March 20th, 2003 and on March 6th 2013 because Nureyev was born in March. A featured movie about Rudolf Nureyev is to be released under the title "The White Crow" in 2019. [173] [174]

[170] Watson, P., Nureyev: A Biography, p.455
[171] Watson, P., Nureyev: A Biography, p.455
[172] Roslyn Sulcas (11 December 2013). "At a French Museum, Peeks at Nureyev's World") New York Times. Retrieved 16 December 2013.
[173] Tribute to Rudolf Nureyev - Ballet de l'Opéra de Paris (2012-2013 season), Homage to Rudolf Noureev, ballet director Brigitte Lefèvre explains why
[174] Vennard, Martin (2018-09-30). "How dance legend Nureyev continues to Inspire". BBC News. Retrieved 2018-09-30.

Saying Hello at the Roxy

When I am thinking about one of the most memorable events in my life, then this would be my first night at the Roxy in New York in July 1998. I was 24 years old when I started going out on the scene. There was not much happening in my university town Hanover in Germany which was probably a good thing, because I had a huge appetite for fun. I was young, I was a student, and I had so many things going for me. I had worked hard to save the money for that summer in the States in 1998. And I knew that it would be a good one.

When I look back, then I think that I was destined to find my second home at the Roxy. I met many people on the dance floor when I was the new boy in town, and some of them became good friends of mine. The bartender Kathy and I are still in contact some 20 years later and her colleague Jose even attended my daughter`s baptism in 2015 and whenever I was in town for a visit or one of my internships, I was found at the Roxy on a Saturday night – young, beautiful and fun loving.

The famous night club Roxy NYC (sometimes called The Roxy) was located at 515 West 18th Street in Chelsea in New York City and started as a roller-skating rink and roller disco in 1978 and was referred to by many as the "Studio 54 of roller rinks". [175]

When the popularity of skating began to fade away the place was revamped and turned into a dance club in June 1982 and featured a mash-up of all music styles from early hip hop, electro, funk, soul, disco, rock, punk, and electronic dance music. Many recording artists, producers, and remixers considered the racially mixed clientele and cross-cultural ethos as the ideal crowd for dance floor tests and the first commercially released record made on a computer in the United States "AEIOU Sometimes Y" was first played there. [176]

---

[175] Steve died in 2012. Cf. "Obituary: Steven GREENBERG", *The New York Times*, March 15, 2012

[176] https://en.wikipedia.org/wiki/Roxy_NYC#cite_note-1

The nightclub hosted one of the largest gay parties "Roxy Saturdays" promoted by John Blair Promotions where many famous DJs such as Junior Vasquez, Many Lehman, Victor Calderone, David Guetta, Paul van Dyk, Offer Nissim and Peter Rauhofer kept the crowd dancing until brunch time on Sunday mornings. Some of the most popular and wanted recording artists performed there such as Cher, Madonna, Beyonce, Mariah Carey, Whitney Houston, Liza Minnelli, Donna Summer, Cyndi Lauper, Grace Jones, Yoko Ono, LL Cool, Bette Midler, and Gloria Gaynor. [177]

I was standing next to the bar on that hot summer night in July 1998 and waiting to order a drink, when the bartender finally came. I was aware that it would be a long night and I wanted to get back on the dance floor when he was suddenly standing next to me. He wasn't new on the scene which is why he probably wasn't that excited about that night and that club anymore and instead thought "same people, same parties, same everything". He knew all about the seemingly endless pressures of being heir to his family's fortune and he also knew all about the privileges which however had led to certain boredom in his existence. He was standing at the bar, and one of the dealers asked him if he wanted to bump it up, when he spotted me and asked the guy with a firm voice to leave him alone.

He was always hoping to meet people, who were like a fresh breeze and who didn't care about his last name or his family background. When he noted me as the new guy on the scene, he smiled. There were we standing next to each other such as hand delivered by faith. The American was full of optimism and gave the bartender a sign that he would cover my drink. Later on, we discovered that we weren't without our own surprises.

He was very handsome and confident; he had the kind of confidence, which people obtained while they were growing up with money. He looked good in his pants and his shirt and like the majority of the guys on the scene was most likely hitting the gym seven days a week. But there was something different

---

[177] https://en.wikipedia.org/wiki/Roxy_NYC#cite_note-1

about him. From the very beginning, he didn't strike me as a typical party boy, who was ridden hard and put away wet like one of those racehorses his father used to own and like most of those guys in that club.

"I can't accept that!" "You can get the next one," was his response with this big smile on his face. I grabbed my drink and introduced myself. "It's Josh," responded the American and raised his glass, "this is to chance meetings and an unforgettable summer." He was drinking club soda all night, and I asked him, if he wasn't drinking any alcohol. "I used to epically", he paused and then admitted: "It is nice meeting someone who never knew the old me!" "I know that feeling!"

Josh Fenton and I had grown up so differently. But we also had certain things in common. We were both keen to win our distance from our dominating parents, our father's unrealistic expectations, our mother's disapproving eyes and by the people's perception what it meant to be part of a specific society. We didn't want to be limited by that until to the rest of our life. We were both ready to break away, free to live and free to love.

Both of us had talked for almost the entire night, and Josh came across as a very considered and kind man and a far cry from many people who I met in New York City later on. We decided to leave and walked down the stairs of the nightclub at the end of the night. "Derek, I am heading your way. Do you need a ride?" "Thank you, maybe next time!" "Yeah, maybe next time. But it doesn't have to be next time. Or do you have another place where you have to be?" I looked at Josh and paused. When the door of the night club opened, we were standing right on 18th Street. The sun was rising on the other side of the city and a brand-new day was about to start.

I looked at the sun rising above the city when Josh questioned: "Are you admiring your sunrise, Derek Meyer?" "I am saying hello", was my response, when I looked at the guy from the Hamptons. I smiled and realized that this was New York City and this was the time to feel alive. I strongly felt that certain people could have an impact on our lives and I did believe in chance encounters and that we meet certain strangers for certain reasons. And when I asked Josh, if he wanted to go for breakfast at that dinner on 18th Street and 10th Avenue, which became one of my daughters' favorite diners some 20 years later, he responded:" I would like that very much, Derek Meyer!"

AIDS in the 2000s – The hopeful years

I moved to London after completing my studies in Germany on January 1st, 2001, which was another attempt to get closer to New York City and further away from my parents. And deep down I wanted to get on with my life and make the most of it. I was hungry and determined to find a career at the stock exchange in London and make it in the United Kingdom even if the country was about to go into a deep recession. And I was confident that I would find love and happiness in the Londoner community despite the thought that real love was waiting for me in New York City, which was a constant reminder and overshadowed my new beginnings in London from the start.

One of the other significant challenges, which I was facing was that I had arrived in that expensive city without any connections. It took only four weeks before I ran out of money and found myself sleeping in a bunk bed in a hostel at Earls Court, where I became friends with other expats from all over the globe.

I took on a job in a hospital to be able to pay my bills while I kept looking for that breakthrough opportunity in finance, which I expected would change not just my career but also everything else. It is fair to say that I had had higher hopes than that before my arrival in the UK, but nowadays I remember those months at the Great Ormand Street Hospital for Children at Russell Square as a rather fantastic experience and associate the right feeling with them that I had helped others during that time.

London wasn't New York, but it was still a fascinating city, where I quickly found my place in the community and became a famous face and frequent party goer. I was probably out almost every Saturday night during the first six years and met many, many people on the dance floors of the city. Nowadays I believe that the thing which protected me most during those wild years were my memories of HIV and AIDS in the 1980s and all the stories, which I had read as a teenager and which had scared me off. I loved the fun, but I never took risks and engaged in unsafe sexual activities, which saved me.

I was aware what was going on around me when I went to the clinics in Fulham or at Tottenham Court Road for my regular HIV tests and where I spotted familiar faces from the gyms at Earls Court and Covent Garden waiting for their appointments. I sensed that many of those guys were quite often there for treatments and not testing reasons in a time when HIV and AIDS were all around me.

They were beautiful people, but there was something different about some of them when I looked into their faces and noticed the side effects of their medication. Being on that medication wasn`t always a smooth ride. Someone could never know before how his body responded to the treatments while an entirely new generation of a younger crowd started to believe that it wouldn`t be the end of the world to become HIV positive since there was medication out there which made existence with the disease possible.

Quite often people`s attitude towards HIV depended on if they had grown up in the 1970s, 1980s or 1990s. I think that I was born at the right time and seriously doubt that I was still around nowadays if I had been born 10 or 20 years earlier. My struggle to find love combined with my belief that it was okay to work hard and party hard would have been a recipe for disaster at an earlier time, when not much was known about HIV and AIDS.

But by the 2000s HIV and AIDS were everywhere. The World Health Organization estimated between 15 and 20% of new infections being the results of blood transfusions, where donors weren`t at all or inadequately screened for the HIV virus. Activists considered it as a rather slow response when the FDA finally licensed the first nucleic acid test systems for the screening of blood and plasma donations on September 21st, 2001. [178]

---

[178] 2000s HIV and AIDS were everywhere. The World Health Organization estimated

The FDA also approved the first rapid diagnostic HIV test kit for use in the States in the 2000s which had a 99.6% accuracy and could provide results in as little as twenty minutes. Medical staff praised that the test could be used outside of clinics and doctor's offices, didn't require any additional specialized equipment and its mobility and speed allowed a more extensive spread use of HIV testing. But while so much progress had been made in the developed countries activists and organizations such as the AIDS Healthcare Foundation were ready to go out to that place where it had all started decades ago and where people were in desperate need of help. [179] [180]

George W Bush and the AIDS Crisis in Africa

We can say so many things about George W Bush. Many Americans and especially foreigners hated the way he was running the country after the 9/11 attacks. People remembered him as some war president who marched to Afghanistan and Iraq while the majority of his people didn't want those wars. There were countless of jokes about the so-called weapons of mass destructions, which most likely never existed and many Americas were angry because Bush had turned the country, which was fighting recessions in most of the years during his presidency, into a laughing stock. But George W showed real commitment when he initiated the President's Emergency Plan for AIDS Relief in 2003, which provided medicine for millions of African people by the time he left office in 2008. [181]

The reality of AIDS in Africa was harsh in the early 2000s. 14 Million Africans had already died of AIDS with another 23 Million being affected and expected to die. More than 10 Million children had already lost their parents during the AIDS crisis at

between 15 and 20% of new infections being the results of blood transfusions,
[179] A Timeline of HIV and AIDS". HIV.gov. 2016-05-11. Retrieved 2018-04-25.
[180] https://www.youtube.com/watch?v=p_2nqK2BoEs&t=26s
[181] Jan 31, Published:; 2019 (2019-01-31). "The U.S. President's Emergency Plan for AIDS Relief (PEPFAR)"The Henry J. Kaiser Family Foundation. Retrieved 2019-03-26

that time. Countless of people were dying every day when South Africa`s president gave a speech at the 13th International AIDS Conference in Durban in South Africa and declared that AIDS was caused by poverty and described the drugs, which were out there as pure poison. [182]

Michael Weinstein from the AIDS Healthcare Foundation was one of the people, who attended that conference when he was approached by local activists in his hotel after the conference. The group met at a restaurant close by and rented a van on the next day to visit different sites and show Weinstein all those African people, who were suffering and dying from AIDS. Michael Weinstein described the experience as heart-wrenching and decided to team up with local activists who were also willing to advocate and convince their government that they had to approach the AIDS crisis in Africa in a different way. [183]

The AHF opened its first clinic in Durban and another clinic in Uganda in 2002 and worked with countless of committed volunteers who didn`t get tired and wanted to help and support people who have HIV and AIDS every day even if they didn`t get paid. The government eventually worked together with the AHF and started to offer medication to their people. Suddenly many mothers were able to care for their children again; they were able to get up in the morning, make breakfast for their kids and help them with their homework, go to work and at least be around until their children reached adulthood. [184]

But the AHF was aware that more work was to be done and started to push the US government to help, which was run by the controversial president George W Bush at that time. But it turned out that the fight against AIDS had been on Bush`s agenda for some time, which became evident when he addressed the union and stated that AIDS could be prevented and that the right medication could extend life for many years. Bush made it his aim to propose The President`s Emergency Plan for AIDS Relief

---

[182] https://www.youtube.com/watch?v=p_2nqK2BoEs&t=26s
[183] https://www.youtube.com/watch?v=p_2nqK2BoEs&t=26s
[184] https://www.youtube.com/watch?v=p_2nqK2BoEs&t=26s

(PEPFAR/Emergency Plan), which became a governmental initiative of the United States to respond to the global HIV/AIDS epidemic primarily in Africa and help save the lives of millions. [185]

Not many people were aware that George W and his wife Laura Bush had started to develop a keen interest in helping people in Africa suffering from HIV and AIDS after visiting Gambia in 1990. Bush described his interest as "compassionate conservatism" and discussed Africa with Condoleezza Rice first in 1998 while running for U.S. presidency. Ms. Rice became his future secretary of state and explained to Bush that the HIV/AIDS crisis was a central problem in Africa and that the United States was spending only $500 million per year on the global AIDS crisis with the money being spread across six federal agencies without having a clear strategy in place. They both agreed at that stage that if elected working closely with countries on the African continent should become an essential part of the foreign policy. [186]

George W Bush succeeded and became President of the United States. When the tragic events of 9/11 happened, and subsequent actions in Afghanistan and Iraq divided the nation George W Bush was pushing hard until PEPFAR was signed into law and 15 resource-limited countries with HIV/AIDS rates being out of control received the majority of the government initiative`s funding. Most of the program`s $15 billion funding was about to be spent on Botswana, the Ivory Coast, Ethiopia, Guyana, Haiti, Kenya, Mozambique, Namibia, Nigeria, Rwanda, South Africa, Tanzania, Uganda, Vietnam and Zambia and another $4 billion on programs in other countries and for HIV/AIDS research. [187]

Just about 50,000 in Africa had access to antiretroviral therapy (ART) when PEPFAR was launched in 2003. By 2018 it is believed that the government`s initiative had saved more than 16 million lives and given 14 million men, women and children

---

[185] Fauci, Anthony S.; Eisinger, Robert W. (2018-01-25). PEPFAR – 15 years and counting the lifes saved *New England Journal of Medicine*. 378 (4): 314–316. doi:10.1056/NEJMp1714773. ISSN 0028-4793. PMID 29365298.
[186] Varmus, Harold (1 December 2013). "Making PEPFAR". Science & Diplomacy. 2 (4).
[187] https://www.nytimes.com/2004/07/14/world/early-tests-for-us-in-its-global-fight-on-aids.html

access to ART with 2,2 million HIV-free babies to HIV-positive mothers. [188]

Since PEPFAR was reauthorized in 2008, it experienced a shift away from the model "Focus Country" and developed a Partnership Framework model to ensure long-term sustainability and country leadership in some regions and countries. PEPFAR works with host nations through bilaterally-funded programs to focus on treatment, prevention, and care for millions of people in more than 85 countries nowadays. [189]

The Partnership Framework enables the U.S. Government, the partner government and other partners to fight HIV and AIDS in those host countries and work on service deliveries, policy reforms, and coordinated financial commitments. [190]

Thousands of Ugandans marched with the AIDS Healthcare Foundation on World AIDS Day a few years later while the AHF had opened a clinic in Cambodia and others had followed. Nowadays the AHF is known as the largest AIDS organization worldwide after the organization reached out to even more countries because people with HIV and AIDS were for example discriminated and looked down in other countries such as India, thrown out of workplaces and family homes without having any entitlements, rights or status in families and societies. [191]

The AHF still focused on advocacy but also aimed to travel to other countries worldwide and set up meetings with members of parliament, prime ministers, health secretaries and those who have the possibilities to change existing policies, which have an impact on people living with HIV and AIDS. [192]

---

[188] https://www.africanexponent.com/post/9281-pepfar-has-saved-millions-of-lives-in-africa-from-the-hivaids-epidemic

[189] https://en.wikipedia.org/wiki/President%27s_Emergency_Plan_for_AIDS_Relief#cite_note-:0-1

[190] https://allstartchoices.blogspot.com/2018/01/when-did-first-aids-treatment-program.html

[191] https://www.youtube.com/watch?v=p_2nqK2BoEs&t=26s

[192] https://www.youtube.com/watch?v=p_2nqK2BoEs&t=26s

Fighting back against greedy pharmaceutical companies

There was this story about this former businessman and hedge fund manager who was convicted on two counts of securities fraud and one count of conspiring to commit securities fraud and sentenced to seven years in federal prison and up to $7.4 million in fines in 2018. At the time of his conviction, many believed that there is some justice out there after he had raised a price for an HIV/AIDS drug from USD 13.50 to USD 750 (5,555%) after obtaining its manufacturing license in 2015. The widespread criticism after the drug`s price increase was followed by applauds after the American found himself locked up for different crimes years later. [193] [194]

Aids organizations such as the AIDS Healthcare Foundation have been fighting for decades against the biggest names in the pharmaceutical industry over the costs of HIV and AIDS drugs and the fact that millions of people in Africa and other countries have had to die while western governments and pharmaceutical companies blocked access to available low-cost medication. [195]

The main issue is that when a pharmaceutical company develops a new drug, then it is covered under patent protection, which makes its producer the only company who can manufacture, market and profit from it. Consequently, the name of the game in the pharmaceutical industry could be called "Monopoly" because in the case of medicine monopolies emanate from those patents, which typically last for 20 years and allow drug companies selling those drugs to charge whatever they want to. [196]

---

[193] https://www.chicagotribune.com/business/ct-biz-martin-shkreli-sentencing-20180309-story.html

[194] https://www.dailymail.co.uk/news/article-3246093/Drugs-boss-hiked-price-life-saving-AIDS-treatment-5-000-cent-tried-kidney-pills-vows-reduce-price-refuses-say-much.html

[195] https://www.youtube.com/watch?v=p_2nqK2BoEs&t=26s

[196] http://www.thebody.com/content/art13653.html

Drug companies are aware of how to get those patents extended and brush of the fact that the pricing of the drug is unrelated to the production costs and instead driven by the calculation of how to maximize revenues. And even if many Western Countries have price controls in place, they usually keep price levels consistent with other comparable countries and drug pricing battles remain one of the greatest injustices in the world. [197]

People who have HIV and AIDS in less developed countries might consider it as slaps in their faces when pharmaceutical companies explain the high costs of their medication with high sums of money being spent on high-risk research and development. It is well known that 84% of worldwide funding for drug discovery research is funded from government and public sources against just 12% from pharmaceutical companies, who instead spent 19 times more on marketing than on basic research while benefiting from government subsidies, tax write-offs and many other incentives the industry receives in the form of corporate welfare. [198]

Americans were outraged when the movie "Fire in the Blood" was screened, and viewers had to learn how much of their tax money funded those research and development programs for medicines which were sold back to them with a majority having problems affording them. Back in 2002, the average annual costs for AIDS medication therapies were USD 28,500 which was more than the average person living with HIV was earning in one year. [199]

But while the high prices of drugs attacked the U.S. public healthcare systems and crippled the AIDS Drug Assistance Programs nationwide, it turned out in the early 2000s that pharmaceutical companies were pricing their products for just the top 5% of the market in South Africa and only the top 1.5%

---

[197] http://www.thebody.com/content/art13653.html
[197] https://www.theguardian.com/commentisfree/2013/feb/22/hiv-aids-deaths-pharmaceutical-industry
[198] https://www.youtube.com/watch?v=p_2nqK2BoEs&t=26s
[199] http://www.thebody.com/content/art13653.html

in India. It was further pointed out that those enterprises are ignoring the rest of the people with HIV and AIDS. Additionally, those giants are working hard to cut off supplies of lower-cost generic drugs originating in countries such as India, Brazil, and Thailand and making sure that they don`t miss out on customers who could afford to pay the outrageous prices for their drugs. [200]

Furthermore, U.S. and European Governments were making use of a number of trade mechanisms and threats of sanctions to impact the supply of affordable medicine in the Global South. The sad consequence is that the vast majority of the world`s people living in those developing countries will never be able to afford branded drugs and unnecessarily die of HIV/AIDS while being denied access to safe and affordable medicine which is produced at a fraction of the prices by well-known pharmaceutical companies. [201]

In some of the less developed countries, the cost of medication for a month was almost double then the income of entire families, which had to choose between food and medicines while pharma companies kept trying to maximize profits. There was a lot of compassion and empathy at the beginning of the AIDS crisis, which was replaced by greed and pharma companies no longer being satisfied with good earnings and decent profits and researchers bringing home a good pay for good work. They wanted much more and aimed to squeeze out the maximum profits with HIV/AIDS drugs. [202]

But Aids organizations such as the AHF were not afraid of fights against the Goliath`s of the pharma industry and banned their representatives to its clinics after accusing them of charging as twice as much in the developing world than other companies do. A march took place on the 7th of July 2002 in Barcelona, Spain with over 10,000 people demonstrating against the high prices of the HIV/AIDS drugs. Other marches followed in Washington DC, Toronto Canada, and Bangkok Thailand. [203]

---

[202] http://www.thebody.com/content/art13653.html
[203] https://www.youtube.com/watch?v=p_2nqK2BoEs&t=26s

The AHF took further steps and started to sue several pharmaceutical companies to force them to lower their HIV drug prices with the first major pharmaceutical giant slashing its prices for developing countries in 2003 under pressure from the AHF and other activists. [204]

[204] https://www.youtube.com/watch?v=p_2nqK2BoEs&t=26s

Gene Anthony Ray

When I look back at the last 35 years, then I cannot deny that Gene Anthony Ray managed to inspire me at all the different stages of my existence. We were both rebels and believed in ourselves and our dreams and proved that it was possible to come from nowhere and get somewhere. When he died, I made the decision to get involved in the fight against AIDS myself and years later I met one of his former friends and colleagues from FAME, who became not just a dear friend of mine but also an incredible inspiration in my life.

The American actor, dancer, and choreographer Gene Anthony Ray was born in Harlem, New York on May 24th, 1962 and grew up in the neighborhood of West 153rd Street. Gene realized his talent as a performer at a young age and took part in street dances at block parties in his community and attended dance classes at the Julia Richman High School and the actual New York High School of the Performing Arts, where he was kicked out after one year. His mother Jean E. Ray remembered that the school was too disciplined for this wild child of hers. [205] [206]

One day Gene Anthony Ray skipped school to audition for the choreographer Louis Falco's movie "Fame," which changed Ray's life forever when he won the part of Leroy Johnson. The film was released in 1980 and a huge success. Just like the character he played Gene Anthony Ray didn't have much professional training at that time but possessed real raw talent which won him the role for the film. The director of the movie Alan Parker was already aware at that time that members of Ray's family were dealing with drugs during the filming, which wasn't pretty and therefore he approached Gene very carefully. [207]

---

[205] https://www.telegraph.co.uk/news/obituaries/1447138/Gene-Anthony-Ray.html
[206] Wloszczyna, Susan (September 22, 2009). "The 'Fame' gang: Gene Anthony Ray". USA Today.
[207] Baltrip, Kimetris N. (November 19, 2003). "Obituary: Gene Anthony Ray, 41 Dancer in Fame". The New York Times.

Gene Anthony Ray was one of the original four actors who starred in the television series based on the original movie, which was produced by MGM from 1982 to 1987 and syndicated from 1983 to 1987. Gene Anthony Ray appeared in the "Weather Girls music video "Well-A-Wiggy" in 1982 and was also on tour with the other cast members from Fame in the UK, where the cast was greeted like the Beatles back in the days and performed at ten venues including a sellout performance at Royal Albert Hall. [208]

He played the role of Billy Nolan in the musical adaptation of "Carrie" by Stephen King in Stratford-Upon-Avon and on Broadway in 1987 and appeared in the movie Out of Sync in 1995, which was directed by his Fame co-star Debbie Allen and in the 1996 Whoopi Goldberg comedy "Eddie" for which he was credited as associate choreographer. [209] [210]

Gene appeared in commercials for Dr. Pepper and Diet Coke. His last video project was the one-hour documentary "Fame Remember My Name," which was taped in Los Angeles in 2003 and produced by the BBC, which brought the original cast members together for a reunion in Debbie Allen`s Dance Academy in Culver City. [211]

Like most of the other actors, Ray struggled to maintain the level of success and fame once the series finished in 1987. His struggle with addictions were holding him back, and he remained a frequent party goer. Gene Anthony Ray`s health consequently started to fall apart after his attempt to launch a Fame-style dance school in Milan failed. Ray was diagnosed HIV positive in 1996 and died on November 14th, 2003 at the age of 41 from the complications of a stroke which he had suffered earlier that year in June. [212]

---

[208] The Kids from Fame Live in the U.K." Fame Episode Guide 5.
[209] Carrie". Internet Broadway Database. Retrieved December 13, 2016.
[210] Full cast and crew: other crew". IMDb.
[211] Baltrip, Kimetris N. (November 19, 2003). "Obituary: Gene Anthony Ray, 41 Dancer in Fame". The New York Times.
[212] Byrne, Bridget (November 19, 2003). "Fame's "Leroy" Dies". E! News. Retrieved 2006-05-19.

But what did Gene Anthony Ray's colleagues think of him? Carlo Imperato stated in the BBC documentary that Fame was Gene for him and Valerie Landsburg remembered that when she first met Gene, she had never seen anybody with more raw talent ever and added that even untrained he was comfortable as an actor, and he was comfortable as a singer. Debbie remarked that he was this amazing ball of energy and fire that was sweet and sour at the same time. Lee Curreri described Gene Anthony as an energizing bunny, and Erika Gimpel had so much admiration for Gene Anthony Ray. Lee added that Gene Anthony Ray had that physique that was amazing before people started doing steroids and joked that he lived on Butterfinger bars and complete junk food and the kind of food others ate who just got wider. [213]

The British press had already announced in 1993 that Gene Anthony Ray was dying and cast members remembered that they had learned about his death numerous times while he was still very much alive and added that he is was still kicking in 2003, maybe not as high anymore but still kicking. [214]

They all kept in contact over the years and reunited once again for the Fame documentary of the BBC in 2003 when they all shared many memories with each other. Both Erika Gimpel and Gene Anthony Ray went to the original High School for the Performing Arts in Manhattan, New York, which the movie and the TV series were based on. Gene remembered that they had to do ballet and the classics in the morning and all the academics in the afternoon. The energy and passion and people's excitement were the same there, and the dancers were always dancing in tights in the school and on the streets of New York City. People let loose during lunch, and it was a very high energy time. There was lots of spontaneous jamming going on because people had their instruments and it was easy to go into a room and try out a new song which somebody had written. [215]

[213] https://www.youtube.com/watch?v=-XcvAFci6pw
[214] https://www.youtube.com/watch?v=-XcvAFci6pw
[215] https://www.youtube.com/watch?v=-XcvAFci6pw

Erika Gimpel remembered that Gene did go to the High School of Performing Arts for one year and wanted to let Gene tell the entire story about that incident. Gene Anthony Ray smiled when he admitted that he was kicked out of the High School of Performing Arts and explained that he never had a problem with the kids but with authority and the teachers. Gene added that his mouth was his problem and another cast member even believed to remember that he was kicked out of the school for slapping a teacher. Gene remembered that getting up early to do a plie at 7 am in the morning wasn`t his thing and that he preferred to see them at ten instead.

The cast members were brought together on that day at the Debbie Allen Dance Academy for the first time in 20 years to remember their on and off-screen adventures and perform their highest success "Starmaker" and explained that the episode behind the song actually hit a real-life tragedy of an actor leaving the series. [216]

Debbie remembered that at that time they were losing one of their cast members and actors who was dying of cancer. His name was Michael Thomas, and that was his last episode. In the show, he was leaving the school, but in real life, he really couldn`t work at that point anymore. The actor knew that he was very sick and everyone standing around of him in that episode was showing him how much he meant to them. Many of them had learned on that day that he wouldn`t come back and the tears were real. [217]

That was back in 1983 when they filmed that episode with Michael Thomas and some 20 years later Gene Anthony Ray was standing with Debbie, Erika, Valerie, Lee, and Carlos at that piano in Debbie Allen`s Dance Academy in Culver City and wasn`t aware that he was about to join Michael Thomas in heaven a couple of months later himself. [218]

---

[216] https://www.youtube.com/watch?v=-XcvAFci6pw

[217] https://www.youtube.com/watch?v=-XcvAFci6pw

[218] Byrne, Bridget (November 19, 2003). "Fame's "Leroy" Dies". E! News. Retrieved 2006-05-19.

I was an MBA student at the European School of Economics in London and worked fulltime to finance my studies and internships in New York when I was sitting in that office in Uxbridge, UK and read about Gene's death. I remember how sad I was and I remembered the years when I was a teenager on that farm in Germany and realized through the TV series Fame and Gene's character Leroy Johnson that it was alright to be different as long as we worked hard and believed in ourselves and our dreams.

Gene Anthony Ray's death affected me profoundly and was followed by the news a few weeks later that my own body had been exposed to a different kind of infection and that I had to change my lifestyle if I wanted my body to get rid of that infection again. Suddenly I was sick myself, and I will never forget the evening when I was sitting in that clinic in London on December 8th, 2003.

I waited for the results of my blood test and was nervous. I had already learned through a letter that something was wrong and that one of my test results had come back as possible. There were only two possible outcomes, and I kept praying that it wasn't HIV. My prayers were heard, and I would be HIV negative until the current day. But being exposed to that kind of fear and having to deal with my health issue made me want to do something and fight not just for myself but also for other people.

A few months later I launched my magazine called "Modern Life Magazine," which brought the straight and gay communities together. My friends and many others supported my venture; there was Darren who was hoping to move into professional photography one day and who was in charge of producing pictures, which were added to stories, which were written by other friends of mine. The magazine had a strong focus on HIV and AIDS and gave people with HIV a real platform to write about their own experience.

We had our first magazine party on my 30th birthday on April 8th, 2004 at the Edge in London and even if the magazine never became a commercial success it was considered as a great and life-changing experience for the people who were involved with it. We were also using the parties to raise funds for the fight against HIV and AIDS and teamed up with charities in London, who were actively supporting people suffering from the disease.

When my career in finance took off after completing my MBA studies, and I found myself working 60 hours a week at the investment bank Morgan Stanley I decided in the following year to move on. But I remained friends with many of my former colleagues from the Modern Life Magazine times, and I knew that people like Gene Antony Ray inspired me at a later stage to continue that fight against HIV and AIDS which we had started after his death.

My own body cleared the "other" infection in summer 2004, and I believe that my ambition and drive to make a difference and help other people had contributed to that recovery. I was very much involved with that topic at that time when I spent time in that clinic at Tottenham Court Road for my regular appointments and asked professionals questions. I also saw people with AIDS waiting in the same waiting room like myself, and while I eventually did not have to return anymore after my recovery, their destiny remained uncertain.

On January 21st, 2005 the Center for Disease Control and Prevention recommended anti-retroviral post-exposure prophylaxis ("PEP") for people, which were exposed to HIV from rapes, accidents or occasional unsafe sex or drug use. People who believed that they were exposed to HIV had 72 hours to start the emergency drug treatment for the next 28 days, which had been recommended since 1996 for health care workers who had been stuck with a needle, splashed blood in their eyes or were exposed in some other work-related way. [219]

Being on PEP wasn't anything unusual back at that time. But while the Londoners were aware of that option and drug, which was offered for free and at no costs by the Londoner clinics,

---

[219] https://www.cdc.gov/mmwr/preview/mmwrhtml/rr5402a1.htm

many people were not aware of the drug in New York or chose not to take advantage of it and save the USD 800, which were the price of the mediation at that time. The lack of advertising in the States led to many people not asking for help when they were exposed to HIV and lives weren't saved by it.

Friends who were on PEP talked about the side effects and felt that they had the flu for 28 days. They had to take seven pills in the morning and seven tablets in the evening, which made them feel sick from the first day on and which gave them a bitter taste, what people with HIV and AIDS had to go through on an ongoing basis. But I never heard about anybody being diagnosed with HIV 3 months after completing the 28 days emergency treatment and hope that this section of the book will inspire my readers to ask for PEP if they should ever find themselves in a situation like some of us did or educate others about it and ultimately help save lives.

Test, Treat and Prevent

Michael Weinstein and his colleagues from the AIDS Healthcare Foundation realized that many people in the world weren't aware if they were HIV positive a few years ago because testing wasn't convenient enough and AIDS tests in California weren't available unless people went to a clinic between 9 to 5 Mondays to Fridays. The program "Test and Treat" started in the late '90s and was based on the idea to test as many people as possible and get those who were HIV positive quickly into treatment programs and not just save their life by providing them with proper medications but also prevent them from spreading HIV to others. [220]

To make HIV tests more accessible the AHF started to offer testing in their Out of the Closet Thrift Stores and also opened a coffee house where everybody could get tested right in the middle of West Hollywood every night until midnight, which changed testing radically. But the main problem was that it still

---

[220] https://www.youtube.com/watch?v=p_2nqK2BoEs&t=30s

took two weeks at that time until test results were available. Even if people dared to go and take those tests they sometimes didn`t come back for the test results since the two weeks waiting period was just too agonizing for them. Things changed, and people who would not have returned were no longer lost, when the fingerprint test was launched, which just took 1 minute and enabled people to find out about their HIV status within 5 minutes. [221]

One of the many things, which made the AHF a great organization from the very beginning was their understanding of the importance of compassion. Running a healthcare system will always require the ability to deal with the technical aspects but also a keen sense for cheerleading, encouragement, and empowerment and the human touch being the essence of what people needed who wanted to help others. And the AHF understands how to encourage people to get tested, to obtain and take the medication and show up for their appointments. All that is the lifeblood of an organization like the AHF.

The AIDS Healthcare Foundation started to focus on prevention after implementing the test and treat model across the world and decided to manufacture and distribute free condoms. But the AHF went further than that and created an in-house marketing department to influence society through changing the culture and encourage people out there to have safer sex. Saver sex messages, advocacy campaigns, and HIV testing and treatment messages were launched worldwide. The organization`s intention was no longer to get people tested and treated but also to create awareness in a time when AIDS was no longer on the front pages of newspapers, and some people put their desire for unprotected sex before their own and other`s people health.

The AHF also criticized dating apps and countless of websites for promoting a hookup culture and spread of sexually transmitted diseases and ran marketing campaigns in the form of billboards, commercials or online campaigns to make a

---

[221] https://www.youtube.com/watch?v=p_2nqK2BoEs&t=30s

difference. The organization was indeed not afraid of rather controversial contents and messages such as "Cheating – Use a condom --- Cheated on – Get tested!" [222]

Is there a cure?

There is this story about the American Timothy Ray Brown who is also known as the "Berlin" patient. Brown was suffering from both HIV and leukemia when he underwent a stem cell transplantation in Berlin to treat his leukemia in 2007. The donor of the stem cells had a cell mutation known as "CCR5 Delta 32" which made the individual immune to HIV. It is believed that roughly less than 1% of Caucasians in Northern and Western Europe are born with this inherited mutation, which is even rarer in other cultures. The resistance to HIV infections was due to a genetic profile which led to the CCR5 co-receptor being absent from the donor`s cells, which makes it impossible for HIV to use CCR5 as its docking station to enter and infect CD4 cells. [223]

Most of Brown`s immune cells and total body irradiation had been destroyed by the chemotherapy treatment. He took immunosuppressive drugs to prevent a rejection of the stem cells for 38 months after the transplant and experienced a miracle when during the 38 months follow-up period the donor`s CD4 cells repopulated, which was accompanied by the complete disappearance of Brown`s CD4 cells, which led to a CD4 count of a healthy adult of the same age two years later. [224]

Brown received the same transfer again in 2008 when leukemia relapsed and discontinued using the antiretroviral medication. In 2010 researchers failed to detect HIV in Brown`s blood or various biopsies and levels of HIV specific antibodies in his blood had also declined which suggested that functional HIV

[222] https://www.youtube.com/watch?v=p_2nqK2BoEs&t=30s
[223] Mary Engel (February 20, 2019). "Timothy Ray Brown: The accidental AIDS icon". Fred Hutch. Retrieved March 4, 2015.
[224] Allers, K.; Hutter, G.; Hofmann, J.; Loddenkemper, C.; Rieger, K.; Thiel, E.; Schneider, T. (2010). "Evidence for the cure of HIV infection by CCR5 32/ 32 stem cell transplantation". Blood. 117 (10): 2791–2799.

may have been eliminated from his body. Eleven years later after he received the donor`s stem cells, doctors still cannot find HIV in his system. Many believed until 2019 that this made Brown the only person in the world, which was cured of HIV. But can HIV and AIDS be cured with the transplantation of stem cells and can the treatment be replicated to develop a cure for HIV which works and can be available for everyone? [225]

Even if Brown seems to have been cured of the HIV infection, it was already after the transfer doubtful that it was possible to use the procedure for many other cases. The method would make it necessary to destroy a patient`s longer-lived cells with a grueling and lengthy chemotherapy and replace them with donor cells, which required the need to find CCR5-matched bone marrow transplants. [226]

Even if the treatment was ever proven to be successful in other cases, then it was expensive and most likely be reserved for patients with no remaining treatment options or cancer requiring bone marrow or stem cell transfer. Furthermore, many questions remained in regards of the reasons for the miracle outcome and people questioned if Brown`s recovery was either due to unusual nature of the stem cells, which he had received or the "graft-versus-host-disease" which he was initially suffering from. Brown was also dealing with transplant complications, which could have been potentially fatal and neurological problems had led to temporary blindness and memory loss and personality changes. [227]

The hopes of millions were dashed in 2013 when people started to seriously question if it was possible to cure HIV with bone marrow transplants. Two patients from Boston, which had received bone marrow transplants with cells that were not resistant to HIV seemed to be free of the virus for months after stopping antiretroviral medications before the virus rebounded in

[225] http://www.aidsmeds.com/articles/hiv_aids_stemcell_2042_14199.shtml
[226] http://www.aidsmap.com/Stem-cell-transplant-has-cured-HIV-infection-in-Berlin-patient-say-doctors/page/1577949/
[227] http://www.aidsmap.com/Stem-cell-transplant-has-cured-HIV-infection-in-Berlin-patient-say-doctors/page/1577949/

both Boston patients, which was disappointing but also not entirely unexpected since they didn`t receive the same treatment as Brown. [228]

It remains unclear, if the Boston patients were ever free of HIV after their transplants or if the virus was hiding somewhere else in the men`s bodies. Further studies also showed that viral rebounds can happen at any time even months after stopping therapy and that people had to be followed very carefully over a long period. Questions were raised, if the patients were temporarily cured by a common complication of stem cell transplants, in which transplanted cells attack the body`s immune cells, which had eliminated HIV infected cells. [229]

So after all, was there a real cure for HIV in the 2000`? It didn`t seem that there was and the HIV reservoir seemed deeper and more persistent than previously known and the current standards of fighting HIV were not sufficient enough to confirm if long-term HIV remission was possible after antiretroviral therapies stop. However, the patients who participated in those studies are known as incredible brave since their heroic sacrifices enabled researchers to learn from their participation which shaped future research agendas. [230]

---

[228] https://www.scientificamerican.com/article/hopes-dashed-for-hiv-cure/
[228] https://www.scientificamerican.com/article/hopes-dashed-for-hiv-cure/
[228] https://www.scientificamerican.com/article/hopes-dashed-for-hiv-cure/

The night at the Boathouse

I always knew that I would return to New York one day and even if I had enjoyed a secure and comfortable existence in London, I consequently decided to quit my job at the French Bank BNP Paribas in autumn 2009 and return to Manhattan, where I had already studied and worked in 2003 and 2004. I took a significant risk at that time since I had to start from zero again when I returned to business school and was prepared to send out hundreds of applications in a time when jobs weren't easily available after the financial crisis.

But even if times were challenging, I was committed to making a difference in my own and other people's lives and was actively watching out for opportunities. I had a very strong interest in the arts and been a regular visitor to the Royal Opera House in London, where I enjoyed all the major ballet performances. And one of the reasons why I returned to New York was that I was hoping to gain similar access to the performing arts in New York, too and get a chance to have a look behind those famous "curtains."

I wasn't naive and in my 20's anymore and had experienced myself that many people in New York were not afraid of hurting each other and quite often took the wrong steps for the wrong reasons. Sometimes things got out of control and fell apart or exploded like granite in people's lives and experiences showed that the damage caused could be real. And one of the major risks and struggles in that city remained that it almost destroyed people when they realized that the love was gone and found their own lives ruined with the ground underneath their feet being torn apart. But sometimes it turns out that the worst is still to come.

I didn't have a strong name when I returned to New York in that autumn in 2009, but I did have a past, and there were certain people, which I could never forget. One of them was undoubtedly Josh Fenton, who I had met 11 years earlier at the Roxy in New York. While I was walking through Central Park on that chilly evening, I had to remember him and the pain, which had been part of our and so many other people's life. I always knew that underneath all that money, which he had grown up with and the pressure and expectations, which had complicated his existence since he was born, was actually a genuine guy who was just trying to find his way. Despite our history and everything that had happened and everything that I told myself I had cared about him until our ways parted.

The Central Park Boathouse was one of my favorite restaurants in the city, and I enjoyed my walk through New York City's Central Park. Both romantics and nature lovers loved the park within the always-eclectic energy that New York was so famous for. The restaurant was designed to coexist with its natural surroundings and the only venue in Manhattan which was right on a lake. Its visitors have been drifting in rowboats about the lake for over 150 years, which became indeed first popular in the 1860s and led to the creation of a storage facility, the Boathouse. [231]

The landscape architect Calvert Vaux designed a two-story Victorian wooden boathouse in 1872, which was twelve feet wide and twenty feet long and which was replaced by a rustic wooden structure in 1924 that needed repair by the 1950s. The investment banker Carl M. Loeb and his wife Adeline donated USD 305,000, and the red brick and limestone Loeb Boathouse was opened in March 1954 and evolved into a landmark restaurant, which offered the option of indoor and lakeside seating and admiring the beauty of the Park while dining on a relaxing evening. [232]

Swedish Princess Madeline and investment banker Chris O'Neil, would have a date here in the following year, which led to a fairytale wedding and three children later on, but I was looking forward to a relaxing evening at one of my favorite spots in the city. Romance was definitely not on my mind on that evening.

[231] https://bikerentalcentralpark.com/central-park-bike-guide/2017/07/27/visit-loeb-boathouse-enjoying-central-park-bike-rental/
[232] https://bikerentalcentralpark.com/central-park-bike-guide/2017/07/27/visit-loeb-boathouse-enjoying-central-park-bike-rental/

"Good evening, my name is Derek Meyer, and I have a reservation. I don't believe that my guest has arrived yet." "Mr. Meyer, that's not a problem, but your table is not ready yet. Do you want to wait at the bar", suggested the girl at the reception. I agreed and took the buzzer, which they handed out to guests like myself and ordered a drink at the bar. I was looking forward to a relaxing evening and smiled until the seat on my right side was taken and a well-known person made me aware of his arrival: "I have the distinct feeling of dejavue. You look good tonight, Derek. Are you on a date here? Do you want me to call that poor person and read that one the last rights?"

I took a deep breath and looked into his face. "Go away. I don't have time for this", was my initial response while I was checking the buzzer and hoping that it would go off any moment and get me out of this rather uncomfortable reunion. "I think you do, Derek. If you go then, I will tell everyone about your little secrets, and I don't think that you want that!" "Who told you?" "It was your friend Nathan, who is apparently also a friend of mine, which makes the whole thing even more awkward and a little weird!"

"I don't have to explain anything to you!" "No one is asking you. I am sure you didn't see that one coming!" I looked at him. There he was standing in his well-fitted suit. I recognized the expensive watch which his grandfather had given him on his 18th birthday. There wasn't a single line in his face, and he still looked good. I paused for a moment. "So, what do you want and why are you here?"

"I am here to try to vow back an old client of my family's business, but he hasn't been around for a while, and right now I am just here drinking to my sad existence. And I want to talk to you about secrets. What kind of secrets? It is funny that you ask!" I didn't ask!" "I think the biggest secret was about your background and your family and there were thousands of little secrets within, and then there was this secret about you wanting a child, which I call the runner up. I remember this wine auction a couple of years ago, where we had that pretty awful red and were talking about us and our dreams and expectations. Was any of that real?"

I think there are a few moments when we have to ask us if we have to blame ourselves for other people's failures and this was not one of them. "Nothing comes to my mind and whatever happened to you is something which you did to yourself. Maybe there was a time when feelings were real and when we could have had that strong bond and relationship. But all that was over when you aligned yourself with your parents and your shallow friends who believed that people like myself aren't good enough for people like yourself. You are looking for something real? You will watch me walking away from that bar, and that will be real!"

"You always tried to save me from my parents and my friends!" "Yes, and you always kept crawling back to them!" "And you were just a boy being obsessed with them!" "No, I wasn't. I knew that they never accepted that farm boy from Germany in their rows. But I am not that little boy anymore, and you know deep down that guys like yourself wouldn't be able to cut it without your trust funds!"

My table was still not available, and I was shaking my head. "I really don't know what it is we are doing here right now!" "Yeah, having an honest conversation for the first time in years really sucks," laughed off the American, "You know I started to realize why we didn't work. We are the same person. We are stubborn as hell and do whatever it takes to achieve what we want, and we don't give a damn who gets hurt on the way!"

"That's not who I am! I got hurt a lot. But I am not the kind of guy who walks all over people and makes their time difficult", stated I and was convinced at that moment that I wasn't responsible for what had happened to him. But he didn't agree with me. "I see you, Derek, I see straight through you. Tell me, who are you hurting these days?" The buzzer was still not helping. "Okay, let me start. Daniel, who was probably the best one, I have been with in years wants nothing to do with me anymore because I am a total ass!"

"We are not friends, and I am not going to prep you up and tell you to fight for Daniel because you don`t fight for anything in life!" I suddenly saw that change in his face and realized that I had hurt him at that moment when he paused. "Ouch!" "Mr. Meyer, your table is ready!" I hadn`t realized that the buzzer had gone off and turned around to the receptionist. "I will be there in a minute!" Before I left the bar, I leaned over and told him: "I see you too, Josh Fenton!" And then I walked away.

My friend and I had finished our dinner and left the table. It was late and hours after the sunset when I spotted Josh Fenton standing at the window and looking into the night. He seemed lost. I thought that I was too good for this world when I decided to stay behind and said goodbye to my friend after he got our jackets. And then I turned around and walked back to the tables in the dining area and to that window where Josh was standing and looking into the dark night.

"What are you still doing here? Aren`t you done trying to ruin my night?" There he was standing with his back turned to me when I remembered the summer on Fire Island and all those evenings, which we had spent on the beach after we first met at the Roxy in 1998. And for a moment I just wished that we had never grown up. Being a grown-up suck sometimes, when it seems that the carousel turns and turns around and never stops.

My instinct feeling was at the Boathouse in Central Park on that night that something was wrong when he slowly turned around. We were standing right opposite of each other, and a look into his face and his eyes told me that he was in trouble. We didn`t need words at that moment. There he was standing with his drink in his hand, which he eventually placed on a table. I took a deep breath and hugged him. Josh Fenton was my person after all.

AIDS in the 2010s – The uncertain years

Is there still an AIDS crisis in the United States in the 2010s? We don't see AIDS on the front pages of the newspapers anymore. It became evident that the notoriously short memories of many Americans had already let them forgotten about the devastating experiences of many fellow Americans in the plaque years when 30 years of AIDS were marked in 2011. Especially younger people believe nowadays that the face of AIDS should instead be an impoverished, dark-skinned mother or her baby in Africa than somebody living and working next to them. It seems that many well educated young urban professionals are not aware of the plague's impact in their own country, which began in the decade in which most of them were born. [233]

Students at Dartmouth College were irritated during a "Plagues and Politics" class that there was a time when AIDS was described as a "Gay Disease" since they had always believed that either inner-city drug users or mostly people in Africa were dealing with AIDS. Activists had fought so hard so that AIDS wasn't reduced to be only associated with gay men, which was a massive achievement at that time. But nowadays many younger gay men are approaching the topic in a different way than their older friends, who had lived through the nightmares in the 1980s and 1990s. The millenniums didn't watch their friends suffering and dying from the disease. They are instead aware of the Highly Active Antiretroviral Therapy (HAART), which has brought so many changes to people living with AIDS. [234]

While many people don't seem to care it is also noted that many older gay men prefer to talk about more pleasant topics then remembering the friends and lovers they had lost or their struggles in case they are living with HIV/AIDS themselves. And it seems that gay men in their 40's, 50's and 60 suffer from PTSD (Post Traumatic Stress Disorder) when the topic AIDS

---

[233] https://www.theatlantic.com/health/archive/2011/12/is-there-still-an-aids-crisis-in-the-us-it-depends-on-who-you-are/249304/

[234] https://www.theatlantic.com/health/archive/2011/12/is-there-still-an-aids-crisis-in-the-us-it-depends-on-who-you-are/249304/

comes up. Just like veterans who had experienced grief and shocks during the wars they try to leave the pain and memories behind, which unfortunately means that the younger generations don't learn about the bravery, courage, and creativity of those, who dedicated their entire life for the fight against AIDS.

Consequently, the lack of interest in AIDS leads to a lack of funding and donations of organizations who care for sick and dying people suffering from the disease. While they receive less and fewer funds from previously generous donors, they are hoping that Latin and African American friends and families of their new clients will provide smaller donations going forward.

The silence of the government back in the 1980s was contributing to the AIDS crisis in the 1980s spinning out of control. And the silence in the 2010s seems to be a strong reason once again, why so many Americans continue to be infected with HIV nowadays. And many Americans are still dying of AIDS because they don't know their HIV status until it is too late or because they don't have access to medical treatments or a stable surrounding needed to use medication correctly or because their bodies are not responding to the drugs. [235]

HIV infections are still increasing all over the States, and there is still a death toll of AIDS in spite of medical advances that have allowed many to live with AIDS for many years rather than being killed off within a few years and in the prime of their existence. Many activists worried already in the early 2010s that cutting back the government's AIDS Drug Assistance Program (ADAP) and international HIV/AIDS budgets to fight HIV and provide research, treatment, and care became the death sentence for people living with HIV/AIDS. [236]

By summer 2011 8,100 Americans across the country were on ADAP waiting lists and hoping to get access to life-saving medications which they couldn't afford on their own and instead

---

[235] https://www.theatlantic.com/health/archive/2011/12/is-there-still-an-aids-crisis-in-the-us-it-depends-on-who-you-are/249304/
[236] https://www.politico.com/story/2011/12/obama-builds-on-bushs-aids-legacy-069587

be exposed to the risk of developing and dying from AIDS or passing on HIV to others. It was believed that in 2011 just 5 million people had access to HAART out of the 33.4 million people living with HIV worldwide, which means that the rest was expected to die of mostly preventable AIDS-related causes. [237]

But even if medication is provided to people living with HIV or AIDS in the 2010s the public usually doesn't pay much attention to the agony they are going through. It is not that simple that when someone finds out about his infections, he starts drugs therapy without experiencing the side effects or setbacks on that therapy. People with HIV and AIDS have to deal with the inconvenience of having to take medications once or twice a day, the burden of having a potentially transmissible infection and its impact on relationships and having to make three, four or more doctor visits every year. And they are exposed to an increased risk for cancers, heart diseases, organ damage, changes in body shape and other potentialities which we are not aware of since a long living with HIV is a somewhat new concept. [238]

People also usually don't talk about the risks and effects on the body of HAART, which is described by many as a long-term chemotherapy, while a considerable part of the public shows more interest in the Kardashians than in the suffering from individuals and communities for which HIV is still the kind of nightmare which it has always been.

So, is there still an AIDS crisis in America in the 2010s after all? It is necessary to ask many people to answer that question. My initial response is "ABSOLUTELY"!

---

[237] https://www.ncbi.nlm.nih.gov/books/NBK236816/
[238] https://www.theatlantic.com/health/archive/2011/12/is-there-still-an-aids-crisis-in-the-us-it-depends-on-who-you-are/249304/

The legacies of the presidents Barak Obama and Donald Trump

It is out of the question that Barack Obama has always been one of the most popular presidents among many communities in the country of the United States and gave the people so much. The Obamas supported gay marriage and were very outspoken in regards of people's rights; and they worked very hard in general to earn themselves a special place in history and have been adored by millions before and after Donald Trump took office in 2016.

But what did President Barack Obama do for the fight of AIDS? Obama had big shoes to fill after President George W. Bush who had positively surprised many activists and spent billions of dollars on the fight against AIDS in developing countries worldwide. Many believe that the Republican who had been mocked as a cowboy quite often set the standards so high for the Democrat that Obama's commitments to AIDS turned out to be disappointing in the years of his presidency.

Activists pointed out a nearly flat funding for George W. Bush's "President's Emergency Plan for AIDS Relief" and a nationwide waiting list for AIDS Drug Assistance Programs with more than 10,000 people since Obama took office three years earlier. It was one thing to make a polished speech or put a statement out and another thing to make a significant difference the way George W Bush did and provide sufficient funding for emergency plans. [239]

The administration argued that Bush and PEPFAR had focused on the global fight against AIDS while Obama was aiming to maintain and refine global efforts and breathe new air into domestic programs and concentrate on providing prevention and treatment for every American regardless of age, gender, ethnicity, sexual orientation, and gender. But both critics and supporters of the president were aware of the severe fiscal environment in the States, which was making it difficult to provide

[239] https://www.politico.com/story/2011/12/obama-builds-on-bushs-aids-legacy-069587

sufficient support for AIDS health charities and aid workers, while 33.4 million people were infected with HIV globally at the beginning of his presidency. Funding shortages in more impoverished countries meant that more than 10 million people with HIV who needed treatment couldn't get access to medicines. [240]

Activists noted that Obama's USD 63bn Global Health Initiative, which was designed to tackle various diseases and build better health systems in developing countries robbed funds from other programs such as the Global Fund to Fight AIDS, Tuberculosis, and Malaria and which were necessary to continue the AIDS battle. More people were worried when Hillary Clinton stated at a conference in Vienna that the prevention, treatment, and care of HIV/AIDS should be a universal, shared responsibility, which sent out a clear message. [241]

But the worst was still to come after the 2016 presidential elections. Over 100 ACT UP NY (AIDS Coalition to Unleash Power, a diverse, nonpartisan group of individuals united in anger and committed to direct action to end the AIDS crisis) activists protested against housing greed and his monstrous symbol of wealth outside of Trump Tower already on October 31st, 1989. The activists were holding signs with "Surrender Donald" and "In NYC 10,000 people living AIDS, only 64 beds", they demanded to fund for HIV housing and called out Donald Trump's tax abatement for building Trump Tower. [242]

Nearly 30 years later the same and many other activists were still not joyful and instead angry when president Donald Trump declared to halt all new HIV infections in the United States within a decade. Trump's statement came shortly after his administration had stripped resources for those fighting the epidemic, cut funding for research and fired the entire White House presidential advisory council on HIV and AIDS, which was an unpaid council of volunteer HIV educators, activists and

[240] https://www.reuters.com/article/us-aids-obama-idUSTRE66M2UG20100723
[241] https://www.reuters.com/article/us-aids-obama-idUSTRE66M2UG20100723
[242] The activists were holding signs with "Surrender Donald" and "In NYC 10,000 people living AIDS, only 64 beds

scientist in December 2017 and only 28 days after World AIDS Day. [243]

The funding cuts of the President's Plan for AIDS Relief (PEPFAR), the Ryan White Program and the Global Fund were announced by the White House in May 2017, which did not just hurt people living with HIV both domestically and internationally, but also increased new infection rates.

It became evident that Trump couldn't care less about AIDS and ignored the fact that there were still nearly 40,000 new infections in 2017 alone according to the U.S. Centers for Disease Control and Prevention and that numbers haven't improved since 2012. Many people didn't believe Trump when he hailed the "remarkable" progress in the fight against AIDS and HIV in his State of the Union speech. Activists shook their heads when the president stated that "together we will defeat AIDS in America" and added that "the only way our world could end HIV transmissions and prioritize proper treatment and prevention is through an exhaustive, across-the-board investment" without providing details on how he was planning on achieving that. [244]

People are upset when they look back at the first two years of his presidency and his actions, which do not just include cutting funding for health research and healthcare but additionally offering support and encouraging staff to refuse to treat LGBTQ patients on religious grounds. The president also totally ignored the United Nations warning from the previous year that the funding crises caused increased rates of new HIV infections which threatened to derail global efforts to defeat the disease and the previously made progress even if the number of deaths declined. [245]

---

[243] https://www.advocate.com/commentary/2019/2/05/donald-trump-doesnt-care-about-hivaids-heres-how-he-could

[244] https://www.reuters.com/article/us-usa-lgbt-politics-idUSKCN1PV2BB

[244] https://www.reuters.com/article/us-usa-lgbt-politics-idUSKCN1PV2BB

[244] https://www.advocate.com/commentary/2019/2/05/donald-trump-doesnt-care-about-hivaids-heres-how-he-could

Bill Gates stated in an interview that Donald Trump asked on two occasions if there was a difference between HPV and HIV. But it was even more concerning and a clear case of employment discrimination when the Trump Administration discharged and fired two service members in the Air Force after they disclosed their HIV positive status to the Department of Defense in December 2018. And people have been even more worried when it was reported that Trump`s Attorney General Nominee William Barr has been holding Immigrants in an "HIV Prison Camp," which resulted with the death of HIV positive trans asylum seeker Roxsana Hernandez from Honduras, who had been in ICE detention. [246]

Activists demand the abolishing of ICE detention and end of the criminalization of those living with HIV in 29 states of the country. They argue that if Trump is serious about ending AIDS in 10 years, then it is time to focus on housing protections, increased funding for housing opportunities and increased employment protections for individuals living with HIV and AIDS, the U.S. expanded healthcare for all including Medicare and Medicaid expansion and a federal rollout of specific education and funding. It is very questionable that Donald Trump and his administration have ever been serious about that fight against AIDS. [247]

Truvada – is the drug the real solution or rather a door opener for the next big health crisis?

Drug companies will always invest a lot of money into public relations and marketing when they push new products on the markets which are expected to be all-time solutions. The San Francisco Examiner reported in June 2014 that the number of new HIV/AIDS cases in the city dropped by nearly 50 percent over the past decade from 532 in 2007 to 332 in 2013 with HIV/AIDS-related deaths also falling by half in that time.

---

[247] https://www.advocate.com/commentary/2019/2/05/donald-trump-doesnt-care-about-hivaids-heres-how-he-could

But the new confidence also came with increased risky sexual behavior, the syphilis rate had tripled and the rate of gonorrhea increased by 50% since 2007 with Chlamydia being on the rise with a 20 percent increase in new cases since 2009. Medical staff was worried that other STDs might not have the same stigma as HIV and that some people consider a gonorrhea infection as an acceptable trade-off for an active sex life as soon as a solution became available, which protects them from HIV. [248]

Many of those people got very excited when The Center for Disease Control and Prevention announced in May 2014 the recommendation of the use of pre-exposure prophylaxis ("Prep") for the protection from HIV, which can lead to AIDS. It was reported that the drug prevents healthy cells from becoming infected with HIV and block the HIV virus from making copies of itself and was recommended to anyone, who had sex without condoms, regular sex with partners who are HIV positive, intravenous drug users or anyone who shares needles. The drug was first described to treat HIV before scientists had another look at it and studies showed that 99 percent of those, who take the medication daily as prescribed were protected from HIV. [249]

At the time Truvada came out the CDC already strongly recommended to use the drug in conjunction with other safer-sex practices including the use of condoms to protect its customers from other sexually transmitted infections such as syphilis or gonorrhea. The prescriptions for the drug jumped from fewer than 10,000 to more than 500,000 within one year, and the likelihood that everybody acknowledged the CDC`s recommendation and continued with protected safe sex was already low at that time.

---

[248] https://www.sfexaminer.com/news/effective-hiv-aids-prevention-treatment-could-be-boosting-other-stds-in-sf/

[249] https://www.advocate.com/health/2014/05/15/cdc-recommends-truvada-hiv-prevention

[249] https://www.advocate.com/health/2014/05/15/cdc-recommends-truvada-hiv-prevention

The benefit of the drug relies on a strict regime. The pill must be taken consistently, it takes at least seven days to reach high levels of protection against HIV for both men and women, and people should use Truvada for four weeks after the last significant exposure if they decide that they no longer want to be on that pill. Most insurers cover the prescription of Truvada to their customers.

People who took Truvada during its clinical trial experienced diarrhea, nausea, abdominal pain, headache and weight loss, and a small segment kidney problems. But those side effects couldn`t stop Truvada's success, which became quickly "the new condom" and led to unsafe practices. For the rest of us who want to play it save it turns out to be a real challenge to find online dates five years later, who are still willing to use condoms while hooking up with strangers and instead are quite often called "condom queens" and other words. [250]

But what did Truvada achieve, which impact was expected to be similar like the one of the birth controls on unwanted pregnancies in the 1960s? And did Truvada become that additional tool in the toolbox to protect people from HIV or a party pill, which exposed people who use it for unsafe sex with recreational drugs to higher risks of HIV infections?

The United States of America is still dealing with a high number of new HIV infections in 2019, and other sexually transmitted diseases are on the rise with New York and San Francisco being expected to become two of the first cities in America to experience a strain of gonorrhea being resistant to all antibiotics while condom use is drastically decreasing. [251]

---

[251] https://www.sfexaminer.com/news/effective-hiv-aids-prevention-treatment-could-be-boosting-other-stds-in-sf/

The meaning of being functionally cured in the absence of actual cures

Most people associate the term "Cure for HIV" with some drug, which completely removes the virus from a patient's body and work like a so-called "eradication" cure. However, in recent years, researchers have focused on a so-called "functional cure for HIV," which does not eradicate all virus from the body and instead get rid of all HIV from the blood and remove any adverse effects, so that patients never develop AIDS or other signs of HIV. [252]

Back in 2013, it was reported that researchers in France identified 14 adults, who had been able to control their HIV infection for years after stopping treatment with antiviral drugs with their side effects, which suggested that certain patients might be able to achieve a functional cure status. [253]

The report was published just two weeks after doctors in the States announced that a baby born in Mississippi had been cured of the HIV infection after it had been taken off the antiretroviral therapy two years ago. The girl was born with HIV and received HIV medication straight after her birth. After the girl and her mother had missed several treatments appointments, doctors believed that she was HIV free and stated that the early treatment had eliminated the virus.

Unfortunately, detectable levels of the HIV returned two years later, which was a massive disappointment for the little girl, the medical staff and the HIV/AIDS research community. It was established at that time, that even an early treatment of the HIV-infected infant did not eliminate the reservoir of HIV infected cells but may have considerably limited its development and averted the need for medication over a more extended period. [254]

---

[252] https://www.verywellhealth.com/what-is-a-functional-cure-for-hiv-3132622
[252] https://www.nytimes.com/2013/03/16/world/europe/french-study-indicates-some-c

[254] http://time.com/2974004/hiv-relapse-mississippi-girl-cured/

While complete eradication of the HIV infection wasn't achieved in Mississippi French researchers highlighted the significant benefits of a functional cure. But what does that mean? Scientists mentioned after the study in France that as many as 15% of people who start treatment early and continue for at least one year might be able to control the virus and live healthy without further treatment and an extended drug regimen as long as they start with the initial treatment within several months of the infection. The French patients had shown early symptoms after their infection, which allowed their infections to be detected early. [255]

The French researchers also remarked that their patients had been on therapy for one to seven and a half years before they were taken off medication four to nearly ten years ago. The scientists pointed out that their patients were in a "remission" status and not being cured since the HIV virus was still present and hiding out in so-called reservoirs in their bodies though at very low levels and remaining undetectable in their blood. [256]

Doctors explained after the publication of the French study that people who were taking the antiviral medications should not stop their treatments on their own since previous clinical trials had shown that the interruption of procedures leads to worse outcomes. Another challenge was to identify and treat patients so early after their infections when in reality people are infected for months or even years before they find out about their HIV status or others hesitate to start with drug treatment because of the side effects of the medication. [257]

One percent or less of people being infected with HIV are so-called "elite controllers," which mean that they have very low viral loads and that their bodies can control the virus without

---

[255] https://www.nytimes.com/2013/03/16/world/europe/french-study-indicates-some-patients-can-control-hiv-after-stopping-treatment.html
[256] https://www.nytimes.com/2013/03/16/world/europe/french-study-indicates-some-patients-can-control-hiv-after-stopping-treatment.html
[257] https://www.nytimes.com/2013/03/16/world/europe/french-study-indicates-some-patients-can-control-hiv-after-stopping-treatment.html

antiviral drugs. It is possible that the French patients belonged to that group and never even needed medications in the first place, which will never be known since they started treatment so early after their infections. However, the French team of scientists called their patients "post-treatment controllers" since they had very high viral loads so soon after their infections and their immune systems differ from those of elite controllers. [258]

The "Berlin Patient", whose HIV infection seemed to be eradicated after he was given a bone marrow transplant from a CCR5 negative donor, was the only example for an "eradication cure" until the news was reported on March 4th, 2019 that a called-so "London Patient" had experienced a similar treatment and recovery. [259]

Scientists considered the cure of the second patient as a milestone in the Global AIDS Epidemic 12 years after the first patient was known to be cured. Since Timothy Brown was cured, scientists had been keen to duplicate that result with other cancer patients being infected with HIV with the result that HIV often returned around nine months after patients had stopped taking the antiretroviral drugs or else patients dying of cancer. [260]

Both patients were given bone marrow transplants to treat their cancer with immune cells modified to resist HIV due to a mutation in a protein called CCR5 which rests on the surface of individual immune cells and which the HIV virus cannot use to enter the cells. Mr. Brown was given harsh immunosuppressive drugs which are no longer used nowadays. He suffered from intense complications for months after the transplant and was placed in an induced coma at one point and nearly died.

Fortunately, the "London Patient" didn't have to go through a near-death experience. He had Hodgkin's lymphoma, and the treatment with immunosuppressive drugs was much less intense

[258] https://www.nytimes.com/2013/03/16/world/europe/french-study-indicates-some-patients-can-control-hiv-after-stopping-treatment.html
[259] https://www.nytimes.com/2019/03/04/health/aids-cure-london-patient.html
[259] https://www.nytimes.com/2019/03/04/health/aids-cure-london-patient.html

and in line with current standards for transplant patients. The London patient quit taking Anti HIV drugs in September 2017 and was cleared and cured of HIV almost 18 months later. Scientists express hope since his recovery that patients probably don't need to nearly die to get rid of HIV. [261]

As of March 2019, there is a database of about 22,000 donors with mostly Northern European descent with the HIV resistant mutation called delta 32. Scientists are currently tracking 38 HIV infected people who have received bone marrow transplants including six from donors without the mutation. The London patient is 36 on that list. Not even the most sensitive tests managed to find any circulating virus in his body, with antibodies still being present in his blood but with levels which declined over time in a way similar to Timothy Browns. The London patient is not considered as forever cured since he stopped taking the HIV medication just 18 months ago, but at this stage, he is the only case to be compared directly with the Berlin patient. [262]

The question remains where to go from here. It is very questionable that the transplants therapy with its harsh side effects and which can last for years will ever become a realistic treatment option for most people with HIV since it is just too dangerous and nearly killed Timothy Brown while receiving treatment in Berlin. This therapy will most likely be continued to be used only for HIV infected cancer patients who need bone marrow transplants.

Scientists are focusing on the development of gene-therapies to knock out CCR5 on immune cells or their predecessor stem cells, which become resistant to the HIV infection and clear the body of the virus. Some companies are working on those gene therapies at this stage, but the challenge remains to reach a modification of the right number of cells in the right place and with precise levels. [263]

---

[261] https://www.nytimes.com/2019/03/04/health/aids-cure-london-patient.html
[262] https://www.nytimes.com/2019/03/04/health/aids-cure-london-patient.html
[263] https://www.nytimes.com/2019/03/04/health/aids-cure-london-patient.html

Another major challenge is the existence of another form of HIV in approximately 50 percent of the people who are HIV positive, called X4, which employs a different protein than CXCR4 to enter cells. Patients with even a small number of X4 viruses are at risk that those multiply in the absence of their viral cousins. There was at least one reported case of a patient who rebounded with the X4 virus after receiving a transplant from a Delta 32 donor. [264]

The continuing focus seems to be on the functional cure, which has been implemented on a broad scale in the following years. HIV testing coverage improved significantly, but the challenge remains to catch HIV infections early enough so that they could be treated accordingly. Until 2019 far too many people have been infected for years before they find out about their HIV infections. More than 1.1 million people in the United States live with HIV or AIDS with every 7th of them not being aware of his or her disease. [265]

The failure of HIV/AIDS medication

There can be different reasons for the HIV virus becoming resistant to HIV medications, which are supposed to prolong life and which can lead to HIV drug resistance in the 2010s including the virus evolving and mutating and no longer responding to medication which had recently worked.

The newly created resistant HIV strains are considered as a significant threat and public health issue, scientists worry that they will infect a more significant number of people because they are harder to treat and expected to spread to other individuals. Activists are demanding increased access to treatment and implementation of alternatives to ensure that people stay in care and additionally push for research and development of new

---

[264] https://www.nytimes.com/2019/03/04/health/aids-cure-london-patient.html
[265] https://www.nytimes.com/2019/03/04/health/aids-cure-london-patient.html

classes of drugs and an HIV vaccine or cure to respond to that threat. [266]

In the absence of an HIV cure, the HIV medications aim to reduce an HIV positive patient's viral load to the point that it is no longer detectable so that the patient won't be at risk to develop symptoms or infect others. Patients who experience drug resistance will have significantly less possible HIV medications available since all the drugs in a given class share the same mechanism of action. As a consequence, a drug-resistant patient is resistant to all the drugs in that given class. [267]

The two types of HIV drug resistance are "Induced" and "Primary" drug resistance. In the case of a "primary" drug resistance, some strains of HIV-1 are naturally resistant to ART drugs, which varies across the globe, and which is the case when an individual's HIV infection comes from an already resistant strain. As a result, the patient begins treatment with already limited drug options, which can lead to additional problems if they develop additional drug resistance. [268] [269]

The other form of drug resistance is "induced" resistance as a result of drug therapy. In the case of induced drug resistance, the majority of the virions are killed off by the drugs. But those virions with the highest fitness will escape the harmful effects of the drug treatments and create an entirely new, drug-resistant population. They continue to reproduce until the patient's viral load returns to pre-treatment levels with a therapy, which had been previously considered as successful and which becomes

[266] https://www.upi.com/Health_News/2016/01/28/Study-HIV-becoming-resistant-to-key-drug/3091454009252/
[266] Drug Resistance". AIDSinfo. U.S. Department of Health and Human Services. Retrieved 31 October 2017.
[267] Clavel F, Hance AJ (March 2004). "HIV drug resistance". The New England Journal of Medicine. 350 (10): 1023–35.
[268] HIV drug resistance report 2017. Geneva: World Health Organization; 2017. Licence: CC BY-NC-SA 3.0 IGO
[269] Freeman S, Herron JC (2007). "Evolutionary Analysis.". A case for evolutionary thinking: understanding HIV (4th ed.). San Francisco, CA: Pearson Benjamin Cummings.

less effective with the virus growing resistant and virion levels increasing again. [270] [271]

There can be different reasons for "induced resistance." A study showed a few years ago that HIV patients in Africa were expected to be three times more likely to become resistant to treatment with Tenofovir than patients in Europe. The results of the study were explained with improper or inconsistent use of the drug, which can be explained by the lack of access to healthcare, stigmatization of HIV and lack of availability of medications due to costs or other factors. [272]

Scientists highlighted that the HIV virus could overcome the drug and become resistant when the right levels of drugs are not taken or taken late, which allows the virus to once again replicate inside the body or spread to other individuals what impacts the general public health and increases health care spending. In 2012 a study highlighted in the Lancet Infectious Disease, which had followed more than 2,000 HIV patients in African and Europe that 60% of patients in Africa and 20% of patients in Europe became resistant to Tenofovir. The scientist explained that the strains of the virus found in Africa was more resistant than the strains in Europe raising concerns about efforts to fight its spread. [273]

As of July 2017, the World Health Organization is implementing a Global Action Plan on HIV drug resistance 2017 – 2021, which is a five-year initiative to assist countries around the world with managing HIV drug resistance. The focus of this plan is on the importance of successful first-line treatments, which affect the virus future response to other therapies. The combination of three drugs remains the most successful

[271] Pascu ML (2017). Laser Optofluidics in Fighting Multiple Drug Resistance. Bentham Science Publishers. p. 119.

[272] https://www.upi.com/Health_News/2016/01/28/Study-HIV-becoming-resistant-to-key-drug/3091454009252/

[272] https://www.upi.com/Health_News/2016/01/28/Study-HIV-becoming-resistant-to-key-drug/3091454009252/

[272] Pascu ML (2017). Laser Optofluidics in Fighting Multiple Drug Resistance. Bentham Science Publishers. p. 119.

treatment as this reduces the probability of the virus developing resistance later on. [274]

There has been much discussion about how to make the ART therapy available to people in developing countries, where the disease was most widespread, and some countries were hesitant to distribute the drugs in under-resourced countries where they worried that patients were unable or unwilling to follow the strict drug regimen. But recent studies showed that individuals in low-income countries were no less likely to correctly follow drug instructions with 77% of Africans and just 55% of North Americans following instructions properly. The results could be explained by the success of community-based approaches such as the HIV Equity Initiative in Haiti, which employed local workers and trained them how to safely distribute HIV medication as well as programs in Brazil, in which generic drugs can be mass produced and distributed for little to no cost. [275] [276]

The number of people with resistant HIV strains are growing and infections rates and subsequent government spending on HIV/AIDS will rise with the progress being made in the global fight against AIDS with the target "90-90-90" threatened (90% of all cases being diagnosed, 90% of infected individuals receiving treatment, 90% of all treated individuals successfully suppressing viral loads). [277]

Activists noted that it requires significant funding to build facilities and improve care programs to help people take HIV drugs properly, which could solve the problem. But the issue remains that this happens in a time when HIV and AIDS are getting less and less attention in the media and governments such as the one in the United States already cut the funding for national and global programs and efforts, which supported the fight against HIV and AIDS.

---

[275] Rosenberg T. *"Look at Brazil"*. Retrieved 2018-11-09.
[276] Dugger CW. "Rural Haitians Are Vanguard in AIDS Battle". Retrieved 2018-10-25.
[277] HIV drug resistance report 2017. Geneva: World Health Organization; 2017. Licence: CC BY-NC-SA 3.0 IGO.

The discovery of new aggressive and dangerous HIV strains

Treatment, prevention, and awareness have improved and come a long way since 1980 when AIDS was a relatively new disease. Back then patients had only one or two years to live once AIDS was diagnosed and considered a death sentence. It usually took ten years before the HIV virus developed into AIDS, which provided patients in the following decades with sufficient time to start with the newly discovered highly effective antiretroviral drugs therapy. By 2015 AIDS is no longer a death sentence as long as patients are diagnosed early enough and before they have AIDS and damage from the dangerous disease has taken a toll. But what if this diagnosis comes too late because of the virus becoming even smarter and more aggressive than it already has been? [278]

Scientists at the University of Leuven in Belgium announced in February 2015 that they had discovered a new highly aggressive HIV strain in Cuba that develops into AIDS within two to three years and three times faster than the more common strains of AIDS. The scientists pointed out that victims started to get sick before they even knew that they have been infected, which ultimately means a significantly shorter timeframe to stop the disease's progression. [279]

Researchers became aware of the cases in Cuba when reports highlighted that a growing number of HIV infected patients were developing AIDS within three years after being diagnosed with the HIV virus. The study also highlighted that a person who has unprotected sex with multiple partners could be exposed to some strains of the HIV virus, which combine and form a new variant of the virus, which is called CRF19.

The latest version of the HIV virus was a mutated combination of three known forms of viruses and expected to be

---

[278] https://www.cbsnews.com/news/new-aggressive-strain-of-hiv-discovered-in-cuba/
[279] https://www.ahchealthenews.com/2015/02/17/scientists-discover-aggressive-new-strain-of-hiv/

more deadly and also more difficult to detect, which causes patients to not seek antiretroviral therapy until it is too late.

Researchers found out that when a patient becomes infected with HIV; the virus will latch on to anchor points of a specific protein, known as CCR5 on human cells, which then allows them to enter the cells. The HIV virus will become AIDS when it latches onto another protein of the human cell known as CXCR4. As of CRF19, this newly discovered HIV virus will move much faster and sooner. [280]

The researchers had analyzed blood samples of 73 recently infected patients, who had been tested HIV negative between one and two years before and noted that 52 of them had already AIDS while the other 21 being HIV-positive with the virus not having progressed yet. The scientists compared the results of the study with blood samples of 22 patients with the more common strains of the HIV virus and noted that patients with the CRF19 virus had significantly higher levels of the HIV virus in their blood compared to those with the more common strains of the virus. They pointed out that the new virus runs out of CCR5 anchor points much earlier and moves directly to CXCR4 anchor points. [281]

Scientists were already worried in 2015 that such an aggressive new strain of HIV could also be found in the United States or other countries on this planet since different types of HIV strain already existed in the States at that time. And they emphasized people to protect themselves in the times of prep and a significantly high number of new HIV infections every year. Activists highlight the relevance to use condoms all the time, get tested every year or more frequently when having sex with multiple partners and if tested positive, get the right care and therapy right away with drugs that are effective even against aggressive HIV strains. [282]

---

[280] https://www.ahchealthenews.com/2015/02/17/scientists-discover-aggressive-new-strain-of-hiv/

[281] https://www.cbsnews.com/news/new-aggressive-strain-of-hiv-discovered-in-cuba/

[282] https://www.ahchealthenews.com/2015/02/17/scientists-discover-aggressive-new-strain-of-hiv/

Researchers have identified 60 different strains of the HIV 1 virus as of 2015 and believe that the newly aggressive form of HIV is created when fragments of other variants of the virus cling to each other through an enzyme, which develops into a more powerful and easily replicated virus. These new viruses pose the next major challenge for humankind, which so far failed to create a vaccine or a cure for the HIV virus, which has claimed 33 million lives so far. [283]

Approximately 34 million people on this globe are infected with the HIV virus, and the latest development shows that this virus is an incredibly dynamic and variable virus, which caused an epidemic which still changes over time. Some people expect a preventive vaccine or cure to be announced within the next decade. But some people doubt that that day might arrive anytime soon for some reasons. And then there are the rest of us who know that we cannot just sit back and wait for the end to happen.

Keeping the promise

The AIDS Healthcare Foundation has achieved so much. When the US government failed to provide adequate support for the AIDS crisis people like Michael Weinstein didn't sit back. Weinstein and others instead protested against proposition 64 or made it possible that hospices were opened in Los Angeles so that AIDS patients could live the last days of their time on this planet with dignity and in a safe and cared for environment. Weinstein lost many of his friends and colleagues, but he and the AHF never lost direction in all those years.

When the organization returned for a global conference to Durban in Africa in 2016, an incredibly high number of people turned up for a march, which was a combination of different walks, which the AHF had organized over the years. It was a huge turnout and celebrities such as Queen Latifah had arrived to support the good cause. The streets were filled with a sea of

---

[283] https://www.cbsnews.com/news/new-aggressive-strain-of-hiv-discovered-in-cuba/

people wearing green t-shirts and many clients, volunteers, staff members, friends, family, and political figures were there to celebrate all the inspiring work of the AHF and so many others for the last 30 years, which had a significant impact on a global level and on global policies. HIV remains a crisis, but 15 years later after its first visit, the AHF made history in South Africa, which was celebrated on that day.

At that time the AHF had the goal to have 1 million people under its care in 50 countries shortly and continued to build programs for advocacy, testing and treatment and travel to different parts of the world where the need exists. The AHF keeps its promise and continues to go to different countries, provide resources on the table, deliver that care, recognize the need to fix the public health system and push for an integrated system on an international basis, which is needed to continue to fight the global crisis and fight what is right for.

The ultimate goal is to stop AIDS by 2030 and people like Michael Weinstein, and the people who support organizations like the AHF will not stop fighting and continue to shake up things and remind people that AIDS is far from over and that we are still in a crisis. And the AHF and other organizations tell us to be part of history, to be able to say that we have changed and saved lives and understand that those of us who participate can take all the pride and know that we are essential contributors when it comes to the fight against HIV. [284]

The largest single-day AIDS fundraising event in the world

When the government stayed silent in the absence of the promised vaccine in the 1980's AIDS activists started to provide care for AIDS patients who were falling ill. Back in New York City Larry Kramer and five other gay men founded Gay Men's Health Crisis in January 1982, which is nowadays known as the oldest

---

[284] https://www.youtube.com/watch?v=p_2nqK2BoEs

HIV/AIDS service organization and first provider of HIV/AIDS prevention in the world.

The AIDS Walk New York has inspired nearly 890,000 walkers for the last over 30 years and millions of donors to support the fight against AIDS. These brave and generous men and women continue the battle of Larry Kramer and those other five gay man who founded the GMHC and first met in Kramer's living room to discuss the new "gay cancer" and raise money for research back in 1981. I will participate in the annual AIDS Walk on May 19th, 2019 for the 10th time myself and I am happy to support an event, which managed to raise nearly $ 150 million for the fight against HIV and AIDS. [285]

I always thought about the AIDS Walk New York as the perfect opportunity to give back to a city, which has given me so much. The GMHC supports 13,000 living with HIV and AIDS in New York City, which remains one of the cities in the country with the most victims of the disease. The GMHC reaches out to those people and others and provides testing, nutrition, legal, mental health, and education services for both HIV positive and negative New Yorkers and pushes for stronger public policies at local, state and federal level to end AIDS as an epidemic. [286]

My daughter Bella who turned four years old in December 2018 has joined me each year since she was five months old and will wait for me at the finish line of the annual AIDS Run, which has been offered since 2017. Bella understands at her very young age the concept of helping and supporting others, and it is fair to say that the AIDS Walk is our favorite fundraising event, which provides funds for the GMHC for the prevention, care and advocacy programs for thousands of individuals and families affected by the disease in the tri-state area. The AIDS Walk New York also supports dozens of other AIDS service organizations through the Community Partnership Program and enables groups to participate in the AIDS Walk New York as

[285] https://ny.aidswalk.net
[286] https://ny.aidswalk.net

fundraising teams, with proceeds directly benefiting their services and programs.

I have felt very passionate about the AIDS Walk New York and started organizing fundraising parties for the event in April of each year in an attempt to raise more donations. Both friends and colleagues have been incredibly supportive, and one of the reasons why I decided to write this book was that I want to make a difference and thank everybody for their incredible support since I first ran through Central Park on that day in May almost ten years ago.

What I enjoy about the AIDS Walk is that so many different people with different backgrounds are coming together on that day and remember and honor those who lost the fight against AIDS and those, who need our support and love. Events like the AIDS Walk give each of us the chance to make a real difference no matter if we are walking or donating money and sponsor the walkers. People always say that they love to help but don`t know how – well this is just one of the many options to make a difference, and since all proceeds from this book are donated to this year`s AIDS Walk you make that difference, too. Thank you.

I have always loved running, but the AIDS Walk remains the only charity run, which I participate in on an annual basis. I was running those 5 miles even before the AIDS Run was offered, which gives us runners nowadays the opportunity to do one of the activities, which we enjoy most. And when the sun is shining, and I pass by the other runners and walkers, then I tend to close my eyes and remember for a moment those I loved and lost.

The morning on the beach

I spent countless of hours on beaches watching the sunrises and being drawn to the solace and warmth which only someone's close presence can provide. Before my daughter was born, I was standing on that terrace of the hotel in Malibu or the beach in Mexico or Spain and be waiting for the sun to appear and for a new day to start. I would be alone, enjoy the silence and have that moment with nature, which tend to fulfill me with beauty and both happiness and sadness.

The decision to come back to the beach house on Long Island wasn't an easy one, and this visit felt different than the previous ones. It was in the nighttime when the curtains in the room were moving in the wind. I was standing in front of the fireplace and starred into the flames. Bella was still sleeping on the sofa and covered by her blanket while a long night was about to come to an end. There was this intense feeling of sadness, and when I turned around to his bed, I felt that pain and uncertainty which so many others had felt before me. I was worried about an uncertain future and not knowing what was about to happen to us after that night.

When Bella woke up, she was still wearing that beautiful blue dress, which he had given to her. The little girl jumped off the sofa and ran to the terrace door, she pushed the curtains aside and ran over the lawn to the beach. His loyal and beloved dog Sam, a beautiful white Labrador retriever, jumped off his bed and followed Bella, while the eclipse was about to happen.

I realized that it was time to go. I walked to the window and the curtain before I paused. I took a deep breath and turned around once more to remember the time which we had spent together. And then I felt that it was time to leave that room and follow Bella and Sam to the beach.

After a while, I was sitting on the beach and felt the sand underneath my feet. I watched the ocean and listened to the waves while Bella and Sam were running around. It was late summer 2018, and I remembered the last 20, 30, 35 years. I remembered the dreams which I had, the ones who came true and the ones who didn`t. I remembered the friends and lovers which I had, which entered and left my life and I once again remembered those that I had lost.

I looked over to the beach house and felt that sense of loss and emptiness. There had been so much loss, but when I saw my daughter on that beach, I also remembered the day she was born. I already sensed back then that from that day on all eyes would be on her and that she is the future. And almost four years later I realized that people like her can make that change, which I was always hoping to make because she is smart, beautiful, kind and the future is hers.

He woke up and realized that we were gone. But he knew where we were, and it didn't take him long to get dressed in his shorts and white sweater and leave his bedroom through that terrace door. Isabela was still running on the beach and playing with his dog when he sat down next to me in the sand. I thought by myself that he looked good and healthy and I wanted to believe that everything would be fine.

"I told you at the Boats House years ago to run, why didn`t you run," Josh wanted to know, "and I told you that I will be okay." I took a deep breath. "Are you still lying to me?" Josh smiled. "I want you to know, Derek that it wasn`t all a lie. Not with you!" "I know, Josh!"

"But I wish that there was a miracle!" "People like you are the real miracles, Derek. "You have experienced so much loss than most of us deemed fair. You experienced the ultimate betrayal through both of your parents, and you lost people you loved, including that second unborn child of yours. But the most amazing thing about you is that you take all that loss and pain and turn it into drive. And despite all of that loss you continue and find joy and happiness as a father, as a friend, as a writer, and as an activist and you live your life right in the face of darkness and make things better!"

I was fighting with the tears and eventually demanded with a firm voice: "I want you to text and call me all the time and I want to know how you are doing. I want to see you all the time, and I want to be there for you if things don't work out. And I don't want to hear about the end unless it is there. And I want you to look after yourself; I want you to be careful and not do any crazy things. Don't do that and don't be a hero. You are my person, and I need you to be around, Josh. You make me brave!"

He nodded and smiled. I hugged him and, we both looked at one of the most beautiful sunrises which we had ever seen up to that point. "Are you admiring your sunrise, Josh Fenton?" He took a deep breath and stated full of confidence and certainty after a while: "I am not saying goodbye!"

The night at the Apollo Theater

We all came together at the historic Apollo Theater in Harlem, New York on November 30th, 2018 to attend the event "Keeping the Promise – One Million Lives in Care: Celebrating Icons of Dance", which was hosted by the AIDS Healthcare Foundation in partnership with our dear friend and legendary dancer, actress, choreographer, producer, and director Debbie Allen.

The evening was an extraordinary way to celebrate that AHF is now providing care to more than one million people living with HIV and AIDS in 42 countries. Those patients are living a fuller life because of the AHF`s excellent work. And we all also came together on that night to pay tribute to the dance legends, which were lost to AIDS. [287]

My daughter Bella had accompanied me to the event, and we were both excited and sitting in one of the rows close to the stage of the theater on the evening before World AIDS Day. Michael Weinstein and Debbie Allen had returned to New York for this evening to celebrate all the things, which have been achieved in the fight against HIV and AIDS since the early 1980s. There was a massive picture on stage, with all of the children, which the AHF treats in Durban, South Africa currently including a 19 years old young man, who was the AHF`s first patient there at the age of 5.

Mr. Weinstein reminded everyone that 35 million people had died of AIDS and that there was still so much work to be done. Michael Weinstein pointed out that almost 1 million people had died of AIDS last year and added that there were 1.8 million new infections in the same year.

Mr. Weinstein remembered that the dance world in New York was hit so incredibly hard during the AIDS crisis and that many of their legends were lost, who would have created even more incredible things if their time hadn`t been cut short.

---

[287] https://ahf.org/wad/

The audience was applauding when Mr. Weinstein introduced Debbie Allen not just as the successful woman, she is but also as an incredible supporting partner to the AHF who gave so much love, comfort and support to so many dancers who suffered and died of AIDS. And Michael Weinstein pointed out that Debbie Allen keeps making a real difference through the Debbie Allen Dance Academy, which supports young people of all different communities and provides them with access to dance.

Misty Copeland, the principal dancer at New York City Ballet, thanked Debbie for being an inspiration to so many people and dropped to her knee to bow before Debbie Allen. It was a very emotional evening when Debbie Allen and her guests paid tribute to the incredible work and talent of dance legends including Michael Bennett, Alvin Ailey, Rudolf Nureyev, and Gene Anthony Ray. Those dance artists are all featured in this book, and their work still impacts my daughter's and my own life until today and a long time after their deaths. [288]

Emotional stories and memories of those artists were shared on stage with the audience and followed by performances by Ailey II, the Dance Theater of Harlem, the Debbie Allen Dance Academy, Syncopated Ladies, and Philadanco. Robyn Hurder reprised her role of Cassie in "Chorus Line," and Jennifer Holliday performed hits from Broadway classic "Dreamgirls" to remember the fantastic Michael Bennett and Jason Samuel Smith reimagined "Beat It" through tab dance to honor Michael Peters. [289]

But I think that what touched us most was Debbie Allen remembering the "Boys of Fame" after the AHF Lifetime Achievement award was presented to her. Gene Anthony Ray, Darryl Tripple, Derrick Brice, and Adrian Rosario were like children to her and nothing hurts more than to bury our children.

---

[288] https://theinformationsuperhighway.org/debbie-allen-hosts-ahfs-keeping-the-promise-dance-icon-tribute/

[289] https://theinformationsuperhighway.org/debbie-allen-hosts-ahfs-keeping-the-promise-dance-icon-tribute/

Ms. Allen wanted us all to take a moment and have a look at the Boys from Fame after thanking everyone for the award.

It was a very special moment when I noticed my daughter sitting straight on her seat and watching that video on stage, which was about those four young men, who had performed in the TV series, stage musicals, and specials. Each of those electric, charismatic boys had brought their style to the screen, and each of them passed away far too young from AIDS. It was a very powerful tribute, and my Bella kept asking me what had happened to the Boys from Fame, which I first had watched some 35 years ago.

I will never forget that emotional moment when my daughter told me that she wanted to help others when she is a grown up. I gave her a hug and a kiss and realized that that famous cycle was closing indeed and that my drive and ambition to make a difference in people's lives already continued to live on in my young daughter at this point.

Fame and the passion for the arts had inspired me when I was a young boy. The power of the arts, the incredible hard work, and talent of those artists and the belief that we can go out there and achieve so many great things had helped me to make it from that farm in Germany to the Apollo Theater in New York City on that night. And I just knew that I will always try to give back until to my last breath.

At the end of that night, Michael Weinstein thanked Debbie Allen, and everyone else for putting this amazing event together and the audience paid honor to Ms. Allen's and Mr. Weinstein's work and all the people, which they had saved. Debbie Allen encouraged everyone in the theater to help if they can help and to take it home and close it out before wishing everyone a happy holiday season.

And then we watched the final performance of the night and all those incredible and beautiful dancers on stage performing to the famous song from Fame "Remember my name" which I had first listened to back in the early 1980s, when the AIDS crisis first started in the United States and which lyrics most of us will never forget.

"Fame, I am gonna live forever. I am going to learn how to fly. I feel it coming together. People will see me and cry. Fame, I am gonna make it to heaven, light up the sky like a flame. I am gonna live forever. Baby, remember my name!" [290]

[290] http://www.metrolyrics.com/fame-lyrics-fame.html

Glossary

A

Accelerated: Occurring or developing at a faster rate than usual

Acquired Immune Deficiency Syndrome (AIDS): A serious disease caused by a virus that destroys the body's natural protection from infections

Anti-Retroviral Drugs: Drugs used to treat AIDS, the virus that causes a serious disease that destroys the body's ability to fight infection

Antibody: A protein produced in the blood that fights diseases by attacking and killing harmful bacteria

Azidothymidine: Zidovudine (ZDV), also known as Azidothymidine (AZT), is an antiretroviral medication used to prevent and treat HIV/AIDS

B

Biopsy: The process of removing and examining a small amount of tissue from a sick person, in order to discover more about their illness

Blood Clotting Factors: Blood clots are a thick mass of blood that forms in a blood vessel and may block the flow of blood in the blood vessel

Body Irradiation: Light or other types of radiation used in order to treat or diagnose a medical condition

Bone Marrow: Bone marrow is the tissue comprising the center of large bones. It is the place where new blood cells are produced

C

Cardiovascular Disease: Class of diseases that involve the heart or blood vessels

CCR5: Protein on the surface of white blood cells that is involved in the immune system

CCR5 Delta 32: Certain populations have inherited the Delta 32 mutation, resulting in the genetic deletion of a portion of the CCR5 gene. Homozygous carriers of this mutation are resistant to M-tropic strains of HIV-1 infection

CCR5 Co-Receptor: CCR5 co-receptor antagonists prevent HIV-1 from entering and infecting immune cells by blocking CCR5 cell-surface receptor

CCR5 negative donor: Donor provides stem cells which prevent HIV-1 from entering and infecting immune cells by blocking CCR5 cell-surface receptor

CD4 Cells: A type of white blood cell, called T-cells, that move throughout your body to find and destroy bacteria, viruses, and other invading germs

CD4 Count: A test that measures how many CD4 cells you have in your blood

Cholesterol: A substance containing a lot of fat that is found in the body tissue and blood of all animals, thought to be part of the cause of heart disease if there is too much of it

Compound: Something consisting of two or more different parts

CXCR4: one of several chemokine receptors that HIV can use to infect CD4+ T cells. HIV isolates that use CXCR4 are traditionally known as T-cell tropic isolates. Typically, these viruses are found late in infection. It is unclear as to whether the emergence of CXCR4-using HIV is a consequence or a cause of immunodeficiency.

CRF19: A recently-discovered and very aggressive strain of the HIV virus

Cytomegalovirus retinitis: AIDS-related eye infection that can lead to blindness

D

Dementia: Broad category of brain diseases that cause a long-term and often gradual decrease in the ability to think and remember that is great enough to affect a person's daily functioning

Diarrhea: An illness in which a person's solid waste is too watery and is excreted too frequently

DNA: The chemical, present at the center of the cells of living things, that controls the structure and purpose of each cell and carries genetic information during reproduction

Drug Resistance: Reduction in effectiveness of a medication such as an antimicrobial or an antineoplastic in treating a disease or condition.

E

Enzyme: Any of a group of chemical substances that are produced by living cells and cause particular chemical reactions to happen while not being changed themselves

Eradication Cure for HIV: To get rid of HIV/AIDS completely and destroy it in the process

F

Functional Cure for HIV: A functional cure for HIV would not necessarily involve eradicating all virus from the body. Instead, the goal of a functional cure would be to get rid of all HIV from the blood and remove any negative effects. In other words, people who had been functionally cured would never develop AIDS or other signs of HIV disease, such as premature aging

G

Gonorrhea: A bacterial infection that is transmitted by sexual contact. Gonorrhea is one of the oldest known sexually transmitted diseases (STDs)

GRID (gay-related immune deficiency): Gay-related immune deficiency (GRID) was the original name for a disease currently known as AIDS

H

Hemophilia: Rare disorder in which your blood doesn't clot normally because it lacks sufficient blood-clotting proteins (clotting factors). If you have hemophilia, you may bleed for a longer time after an injury than you would if your blood clotted normally

Hemophiliacs: Usually affecting only males but transmitted by women to their male children, characterized by loss or impairment of the normal clotting ability of blood so that a minor wound may result in fatal bleeding

Hepatitis C: Infectious disease caused by the hepatitis C virus that primarily affects the liver. During the initial infection people often have mild or no symptoms

Highly Active Antiretroviral Therapy (HAART): Medications used to treat HIV infection and usually measured by survival

HIV: The human immunodeficiency viruses (HIV) are two species of Lentivirus (a subgroup of retrovirus) that causes HIV infection and over time acquired immunodeficiency syndrome (AIDS)

HIV Remission: Refers to the absence of active disease for a period of at least 1 month. The absence of active disease does not mean that disease has been cured or even that there are no detectable signs of disease

HIV X4 Virus: Approximately 50% of late-stage HIV patients develop CXCR4-tropic (X4) virus in addition to CCR5-tropic (R5) virus. X4 emergence occurs with a sharp decline in CD4+ T cell counts and accelerated time to AIDS

Hodgkin`s lymphoma: Type of lymphoma in which cancer originates from a specific type of white blood cells called lymphocytes. Symptoms may include fever, night sweats, and weight loss. Often there will be non-painful enlarged lymph nodes in the neck or under the arm

HPV: HPV is the most common sexually transmitted infection (STI). HPV is a different virus than HIV and HSV (herpes). 79 million Americans, most in their late teens and early 20s, are infected with HPV. There are many different types of HPV. Some types can cause health problems including genital warts and cancers.

I
_____

Immune System: Host defense system comprising many biological structures and processes within an organism that protects against disease

Immunosuppressive Drugs: class of drugs that suppress, or reduce, the strength of the body's immune system and reduce the risk of the body rejecting donor cells or organs

J

Junkies: A drug addict, especially one addicted to heroin

K

Kaposi`s sarcoma: Type of cancer that can form masses in the skin, lymph nodes, or other organs. The skin lesions are usually purple in color. They can occur singularly, in a limited area, or be widespread

L

Leukemia: Group of blood cancers that usually begin in the bone marrow and result in high numbers of abnormal blood cells. These blood cells are not fully developed and are called blasts or leukemia cells

Lymph: A colorless fluid containing white blood cells, which bathes the tissues and drains through the lymphatic system into the bloodstream

M

Meningitis: Acute inflammation of the protective membranes covering the brain and spinal cord, known collectively as the meninges. The most common symptoms are fever, headache, and neck stiffness

Mutation: Any persisting change in the genetic material of a cell. Mutations most commonly involve a single gene but may affect a major part, or even the whole of, a chromosome or may change the number of chromosomes (genomic mutation)

N

Nausea: Unpleasant, diffuse sensation of unease and discomfort, often perceived as an urge to vomit. While not painful, it can be a debilitating symptom if prolonged, and has been described as placing discomfort on the chest, upper abdomen, or back of the throat

Nervous System: Part of a human that coordinates its actions by transmitting signals to and from different parts of its body. The nervous system detects environmental changes that impact the body, then works in tandem with the endocrine system to respond to such events

P

Placebo: Anything that seems to be a "real" medical treatment -- but isn't. It could be a pill, a shot, or some other type of "fake" treatment

Pneumonia: Inflammatory condition of the lung affecting primarily the small air sacs known as alveoli. Typically symptoms include some combination of productive or dry cough, chest pain, fever, and trouble breathing

Pneumocystis: Organism that causes pneumocystis pneumonia (PCP)

Pneumocystis Carinii Pneumonia: Pneumocystis pneumonia (PCP) is a serious infection that causes inflammation and fluid buildup in your lungs and can it can make people with weakened immune systems, such as someone with HIV, very sick

Pneumocystis: Organism that causes pneumocystis pneumonia (PCP)

Post-Exposure Prophylaxis ("PEP"): Taking antiretroviral medicines (ART) after being potentially exposed to HIV to prevent becoming infected

Protease Inhibitor: Class of antiviral drugs that are widely used to treat HIV/AIDS and hepatitis C. Protease inhibitors prevent viral replication by selectively binding to viral proteases (e.g. HIV-1 protease) and blocking proteolytic cleavage of protein precursors that are necessary for the production of infectious viral particles

PTSD (Post Traumatic Stress Disorder): Disorder that develops in some people who have experienced a shocking, scary, or dangerous event. It is natural to feel afraid during and after a traumatic situation. Fear triggers many split-second changes in the body to help defend against danger or to avoid it

R

Replicating: make an exact copy of; reproduce.

Retrovirus: Group of RNA viruses which insert a DNA copy of their genome into the host cell in order to replicate, e.g. HIV

Reverse Transcriptase Inhibitors: Class of antiretroviral drugs used to treat HIV infection or AIDS, and in some cases hepatitis B.RTIs inhibit activity of reverse transcriptase, a viral DNA polymerase that is required for replication of HIV and other retroviruses

S

Stem Cell Transplantation: The basis for stem cell transplantation is that blood cells (red cells, white cells and platelets) and immune cells (lymphocytes) arise from the stem cells, which are present in marrow, peripheral blood and cord blood. Intense chemotherapy or radiation therapy kills the patient's stem cells

Syphilis: Sexually transmitted disease (STD) that can have very serious complications when left untreated, but it is simple to cure with the right treatment

T

T-cells: A type of white blood cell that is of key importance to the immune system and is at the core of adaptive immunity, the system that tailors the body's immune response to specific pathogens. The T cells are like soldiers who search out and destroy the targeted invaders

T4 Count: Count of white blood cell

Tribulations: An experience that tests one's endurance, patience, or fait

V

Viral Load: An HIV viral load test measures the number of HIV particles in a milliliter (mL) of blood. These particles are also known as "copies." The test assesses the progression of HIV in the body

Virions: the infectious form of a virus as it exists outside the host cell, consisting of a core of DNA or RNA, a protein coat, and, in some species, an external envelope

W

White Blood Cell Count: The white blood cell (WBC) count totals the number of white blood cells in a person's sample of blood. It is one test among several that is included in a complete blood count (CBC), which is often used in the general evaluation of a person's health

www.ingramcontent.com/pod-product-compliance
Lightning Source LLC
Chambersburg PA
CBHW030754180526
45163CB00003B/1024